# Everything we know is wrong!

# Everything we know is wrong!

## The trendspotter's handbook

**Magnus Lindkvist**

 **Marshall Cavendish**
Business

Copyright © 2010 Magnus Lindkvist

First published in 2010 by Marshall Cavendish Business
An imprint of Marshall Cavendish International

5F / 32–38 Saffron Hill
London EC1N 8FH
United Kingdom

and

1 New Industrial Road
Singapore 536196
genrefsales@sg.marshallcavendish.com
www.marshallcavendish.com/genref

Marshall Cavendish is a trademark of Times Publishing Limited

Other Marshall Cavendish offices:
Marshall Cavendish International (Asia) Private Limited, 1 New Industrial Road,
Singapore 536196 • Marshall Cavendish Corporation. 99 White Plains Road,
Tarrytown NY 10591–9001, USA • Marshall Cavendish International (Thailand) Co
Ltd. 253 Asoke, 12th Floor, Sukhumvit 21 Road, Klongtoey Nua, Wattana, Bangkok
10110, Thailand • Marshall Cavendish (Malaysia) Sdn Bhd, Times Subang, Lot
46, Subang Hi-Tech Industrial Park, Batu Tiga, 40000 Shah Alam, Selangor Darul
Ehsan, Malaysia

The right of Magnus Lindkvist to be identified as the author of this work has been
asserted by him in accordance with the Copyright, Designs and Patents Act 1988.

The author and publisher have used their best efforts in preparing this book and
disclaim liability arising directly and indirectly from the use and application of this
book.

All reasonable efforts have been made to obtain necessary copyright permissions.
Any omissions or errors are unintentional and will, if brought to the attention of the
publisher, be corrected in future printings.

A CIP record for this book is available from the British Library

ISBN 978-0-462-09966-8

Illustrations by L I N D K V I S T & Co / Lotta Olsson

Printed and bound in Great Britain by
CPI William Clowes, Beccles NR34 7TL

Dedicated to my family
and to anyone who spends their day creating something

# Contents

# Introduction

## Congratulations, you're clueless

*May you live in interesting times.*

– Chinese curse

# What the hell just happened?

Korčula Island, Croatia. September 2008. The late summer is blowing a gentle breeze over this beautiful island in the southern Adriatic. The olive trees are dark green. The water emerald blue. Timeless would be a word that would come to mind if it weren't such a cliché. In the living room, the television is on with my twin infants taking turns to either bite it or use it as walking support. The BBC news is full of drama and tension. Banks are collapsing. The financial system is in freefall. It even seems that capitalism itself is at stake. The contrast between the drama unfolding on TV and the tranquillity in my surroundings could not be greater. This crisis will be described as special in the months to come. Special because it is so vast and affects so many different parts of the economy. Special because of its global reach, its unparalleled scope and lack of repentance in its destructive force. Most of all, though, it is described as special because it was so completely unexpected when it struck.

Over the months following the meltdown, a number of professors, economists and pundits appeared and claimed they foresaw it all. The rest of us – some 99 per cent – were taken by surprise. If there's any kind of beauty – or, at least, a redeeming feature – to this sharp economic downturn, it is the fact that we all realized and had to admit that we are blind to many things happening in our midst. We are blind to the many hidden forces acting behind the scenes of everyday life. We are blind to long-term developments that were initiated decades ago and are only now coming to fruition. We are blind to most things happening in the world no matter how much news we consume. This is a

> We are blind to the hidden forces acting behind the scenes of everyday life

book intended to make us aware of this kind of blindness. It is a book about not knowing. The title – *Everything we know is wrong!* – is not a collective insult but a call to curiosity.

## ● We are all trendspotters now!

Creativity author Daniel Pink claims that we're living in an age that will be dominated increasingly by "creators and empathizers, pattern recognizers and meaning makers". There is one short word that encompasses all four of these activities: trendspotting. Just as 11 September 2001 made French newspaper *Le Monde* proclaim "*Nous sommes tous américains!*" (We are all Americans!), the events of September 2008 made us realize that we are all trendspotters. We cannot entrust our understanding of the world to some self-proclaimed experts in the way Roman soldiers consulted the Oracle at Delphi. The experts had

> We cannot entrust our understanding of the world to self-proclaimed experts

let us down. We had to take matters into our own hands. All it takes to be a trendspotter is to ask yourself the question: "What's going on in the world?" and then pick up a newspaper, log on to a website, switch on the television or ask someone else that very question or a variation of it. It doesn't take more than some curiosity and making the effort to go outside our own heads for answers to add this title to our business cards. This is a book written for all the trendspotters in the world, and that includes you.

## ● Trend – the story behind the word

Originating in the Norse word for "to turn", *trendr*, the word trend was long used to describe the flow of a river or current ("The Mississippi is trending west"). When statistics gained popularity in the nineteenth century, the meaning of "trend" was extended to include definitions of demographic movements and mass observations. The real breakthrough for the word, however, came after the Second World War, when society broke away from a conformist past to embrace individual differentiation. The attribute "trendy" was born. Just as Eskimos are rumoured – although it's never been confirmed – to have hundreds of words for snow, there are many different ways to describe the type of changes we see (and don't see) around us. To simplify matters, a useful metaphor is to think of yourself standing on a crowded city street somewhere in the world. Laid out before you are at least three different kinds of trends:

**There are many different ways to describe the changes we see around us**

- If you look at people at street level, you'll see what they wear and what's in their hands. You may even hear certain words in their conversation referring to current events. These kinds of trends are *microtrends* or *fashion trends* and tend to last between one and five years. These kinds of trends tend to dictate what we wear, what kind of electronic gadgets we use and what kind of buzzwords permeate our language.

- If you look slightly higher, you'll see the façades of buildings. There, you'll be able to track *macrotrends* with a lifespan of about a decade or two. These kind of trends include economic cycles and shifts, political "winds" and the rise of a new kind of technology. These will be visible in the kinds of logotypes that decorate buildings – what kind of industries are doing well or disappearing.

- Finally, if you stare at the tops of buildings, you'll be able to see certain *megatrends*. These are deep societal changes lasting more than two decades and can be seen in the height of buildings (built to house many people because of urbanization, perhaps) or the purpose of certain constructions (the chapel becomes a shopping mall or a mosque, for example).

That's how far our eyes can see, but if we were to travel up into space and look down at the earth, we would be able to detect so-called *gigatrends*. These trends, spanning half-centuries or more, are especially visible at night, when the economic activities in various regions tell us what parts of the world house intense economic activity, what regions are growing and urbanizing, and how cities are growing together into vast megaregions.

In the past few decades the word "trend" has exploded in usage owing in part to an increase in the number of media channels available to consumers. One implication is that the meaning of the word has been further enriched to encompass a number of different phenomena. These include:

- An observation of similarities in a certain place or within a certain period of time. For example, global temperatures are rising, people are living longer and having fewer or more children, and more people tend to wear a certain brand or colour.

- A purchase recommendation wherein an authority figure such as a fashion journalist or a management guru urges people to act or shop in a certain way because it will be "in", "trendy", "hip" or "all the rage" next season. "White is the new black!" "Downsize!" "Visit Paris!"

- Anomalies that challenge the status quo, assumptions or prejudices. These can describe a new or different kind of behaviour or technology, for example, and are often preceded by a dramatic "Did you know ...?"

The inflation in the number of meanings of "trend" can easily create confusion. An example is that it's become somewhat fashionable to proclaim "the death of trends", especially in the emerging environmental movement or because of increased media fragmentation. Statements like these, however, simplify and narrow the meaning of the word down to only one of its many uses. Besides, there are a number of reasons why people have an inherent need for group-ing phenomena together and labelling them for the purpose of description and conversation:

**We are social creatures who long for a shared worldview**

- We are social creatures who long for a shared worldview. To put it in the words of C. S. Lewis: "We read to know we're not alone."
- The explosion in the number of media channels increases the need to group observations together for a more accurate view of world events.
- We are copying creatures, even on a very basic level. If you film people in a room without their knowledge and then play the recording in slow motion, you can track how even the smallest changes in body language can migrate between people as they imitate other people without being aware of it. This behaviour is repeated in a conscious context too, in everything from clothing styles to opinions being copied between people.
- Information is power and potentially money. Acquiring insights about markets, customers and societies is a valuable competitive tool. It's also a great way of excelling in Trivial Pursuit or mastering dinner-table conversation.
- We have a biologically conditioned interest in the future. Embed-ded in the prefrontal cortex – the foremost part of our brain – is the ability to think about the future in abstract ways, using infor-mation about today to shape tomorrow's outcome.

## The future is fuzzy

Just because our brain enables us to think about the future doesn't mean everyone does it in the same way. There are a number of differ-ent ways of seeing the future if we study historic and contemporary schools of future-thought:

- *Utopians and Dystopians*: These tend to view the future as a one-way street into either doom or paradise. Followers are characterized by a stubborn insistence that virtually anything that happens is supporting evidence for their particular point of view.

- *The Pendulum and the Spiral Staircase*: These schools view time as circular with recurring themes echoing continually. The "Pendulumers" see a constant swing between two extremes, political, technological or otherwise. The "Spiral Staircasers" have a similar view but argue that we are on a positive or a negative trajectory. The implication is that themes may indeed return – never in the same form, but rather in an amplified, more extreme way.

- *The Black Hole*: Finally, we have the people who view any kind of philosophy about time or attempt at prediction as utterly futile. Time is a man-made abstraction and randomness is the ultimate ruler of our worlds. Just sit back and go along for the ride.

## A trendspotter never knows

In my speaking engagements, I am sometimes – against my wishes – referred to as "an expert on trends". This is, in my view, an oxymoron. Detecting trends and recognizing patterns rely on an open mind and a continual resistance to jumping to conclusions. To put it another way, as a trendspotter I take pride in knowing absolutely nothing. An "expert on trends" is by definition obsolete. When you *know* things, you close yourself off to new perspectives and ideas. My professional role rests upon two basic ideas. One formulated by a New Age entrepreneur, the other by myself:

**As a trendspotter I take pride in knowing absolutely nothing**

- *An Opportunistic Collector*: The late Body Shop founder Anita Roddick claimed that the secret not only to successful trendspotting but also to successful entrepreneurship in general was to be "an opportunistic collector", to have one's antennae out at all times. This is a fundamental difference between professional trendspotters and, for example, management consultants. The latter work on projects limited in time and scope, and as they do so, they immerse themselves in data and then move on. A good trendspotter will always be on the lookout for quotes, patterns and insights that are somehow revealing of the world we live in or, as in the case of this book, reveal something we may not have previously seen, heard or thought about.

● *A DJ of Ideas*: At an event a few years ago, I was asked the following question: "How come you're not rich if you claim to know so much about the future?" Disregarding the presumptuousness (and it turns out to be an accurate observation), I drew the analogy between my work and that of a DJ. You don't ask a DJ why he or she doesn't play an instrument or sing, because you know that their work is about making people dance. My work, as opposed to that of an investment banker or a management consultant, is about making unexpected connections and moving people's perceptions about a certain phenomenon. DJs make people move. DJs of Ideas move minds.

## ● Be the oracle!

Not knowing unleashes curiosity. While many people search for a convenience of conviction – from religious fundamentalism to political dogma – a much greater world will reveal itself to those of us ready to live in doubt and scepticism. Once upon a time, people relied on dubious, often expensive, witch doctors to acquire information about the past, present and future. Nowadays, we have access to a tremendous number of tools to help guide us into an unknown future. We have to be the oracle ourselves. Or the witch doctor. Or the guiding light. My mission in writing this book is to make you a better trendspotter with an ability to inspire, amuse, move minds and change the world. Read it and go out and tell others about what you see and what you think it means. I look forward to hearing your stories and sharing your world.

**We have to be the oracle ourselves**

Magnus Lindkvist
magnus@pattern-recognition.se
Stockholm, July 2009

# The goal and structure of this book

*Vision is the art of seeing things invisible.*

– Jonathan Swift

## Trendspotting in ten seconds

On a recent visit to a bookshop, I noticed a vast number of titles aiming to help people in a very short time span. Change your life in twenty days. Lose weight in a week. Get rich in less than a year. Not wanting to be outdone, I offer here a ten-second guide to trendspotting: log on to Google and type the word "trends" in the search box. *Voila!* Millions of hits just waiting to be explored. The results will, of course, be mixed at best and based upon other people's ideas about what's happening in the world. If you want a richer and deeper view, keep reading.

## A hidden world

Imagine a secret, hidden world. This idea has inspired most science fiction stories and fairy tales. What if I told you that there really is such a world, hidden in plain view right before our eyes? Before you conjure up images of talking bunny rabbits and Wicked Witches of the East, let me point out that this world follows more or less the same scientific laws as our own. It exists right here, right now, and chances are that many of us have missed it because we don't take our roles as trendspotters seriously enough. How on earth can we have missed an entire world hidden right in front of us, you may ask? The principles are actually quite simple. We humans suffer from something called *change blindness* – an inability to detect even the most basic changes taking place right before our eyes. This blindness may have a number of causes. The changes may be too large, too complex or may have taken place over too long a period for us to notice. Conversely, the changes may be too small or too ordinary for us to think about them as changes. We live in the microcosm created by our brain and that microcosm is not a very accurate portrayal of what we, rather sloppily, refer to as "the real world". Change blindness is why so many of us have been taken by surprise by events like 9/11 or the financial collapse of 2008.

## ● The blind guide

A trendspotter's role is to detect changes in business and society. It was in this profession that I started to consider why some trends are talked and written about while others hardly get noticed at all. It seemed as if people were blind to many changes I had seen, and that I, in turn, had missed things they were telling me about. Initially, I took great pride in knowing things few others did and berated myself in the opposite cases. Eventually I realized that the reasons people had missed certain changes in business and society had very little to do with what kind of magazines or blogs they read. Well-read people are the kinds of people we consider "hip", "trendy" and "with it". There are certainly a number of fashion or lifestyle trends that depend on us following specific media, but these types of narrow, here-today-gone-tomorrow "fads" had never been of much interest to me. I, like many others, am interested in deeper, transformational changes that will alter more than the colour of your shirt and your particular brand of MP3 player. These types of trends tend not to be written about in a single magazine or blog entry but demand that we go deeper, find different sources, have our antennae out, open our eyes and our minds.

## ● Invisible trends

Many people rate their innate ability to detect changes – their trendspotting ability, if you will – as "above average". In the past few years, I have made a point of asking people I meet to rate their own skill at detecting changes on a scale of 1 to 10, with 10 being superior. I've asked over a thousand people in all walks of life around the world, and a majority of these people, well above 80 per cent, rate themselves as being 5+ or "above average". This is akin to those surveys in which 80 per cent of car drivers rate themselves as being in the top 20 per cent in terms of ability, i.e. better than 80 per cent of all car drivers. We want to believe that we are more adept at detecting changes because that particular skill is highly rewarded, especially in the world of business and stock markets. Many of us are wrong, however. We're not nearly as good at detecting changes as we like to believe. The broken lens through which we look at the world is what shields an entire world of insights from our view. It is the kinds of cracks in the lens and the shades of invisibility they generate which will be the focus of each chapter in this book.

> The broken lens through which we look shields an entire world of insights from our view

## ● Seven shades of invisibility

This book is organized into seven chapters, with each chapter focusing on a particular reason why certain kinds of trends are invisible to us. I will illustrate each of these trends with an example that has changed and shaped my worldview in the past few years. It is my hope and belief that these stories will be inspiring and eye-opening to you as well. Besides, you can read the book in two different ways – as an insight into perception or as an insight into current world-changing trends.

The seven shades of invisibility are:

1. *Invisibility by gradualism – The changes were too slow for us to notice!*
Slow, long-term changes are invisible because our brain fails to

register them. If changes span decades, each generation will increasingly adapt to them over time and they will become embedded as a natural part of life. Take environmental pollution as one example. Imagine if signs with "Poison – No Swimming" were erected overnight by lakes or rivers in or near cities. We'd panic and make furious attempts to find the culprit. Since environmental damage has slowly become a natural fact of life over decades, however, nobody raises an eyebrow when weather reports warn of high smog levels or rivers and lakes are too dirty to swim in.

2. *Invisibility by minuscule changes – We couldn't see the forest for all those damn trees!*
Human vision is trained to see things as fixed and rigid when they are really made up of constantly moving parts. Mountains are seen as eternal when they are in actuality constantly shrinking from all the wear and tear of the elements. People's personalities are seen as static except when it comes to you – you can change, but few others can. Because we have this idea about rigidity, we start applying it to markets and to society in general. Organizations define themselves by boundaries and create elaborate mission statements and brand strategies. Industries are given names and borders. People are grouped into clusters. Geographical territories are defined as nations – by artificial borders in the soil. This rigid vision is often erroneous. It makes us overlook changes that might have been taking place right before our eyes. We were so busy watching the forest we didn't notice that the trees had moved on.

3. *Invisibility by suddenness – We blinked and missed it!*
If slow and gradual change makes us blind to change, then at least we should be able to detect drastic and sudden change, right? Wrong. The atrocities of 9/11 were sudden and seen by millions around the world. We were taken by surprise mostly because our lens hadn't adapted to present conditions. The 1990s had been called "the history-less decade" by some and the new wealth generated by the

dotcom boom had made many blind to underlying changes in geo-politics after the end of the cold war. We are constantly surprised by manifestations like these because we fail to grasp the underlying, invisible changes. We focus on the "hardware", so to speak, and miss the "software". This also implies that we may fail to understand how certain changes in our midst, from globalization to the rise of the Internet, are altering our ways of thinking and functioning as human beings.

4. *Invisibility by linear thinking – We fail to think exponentially!*
   We want the world to feel somewhat safe and predictable, which may be one of the reasons we have something called "trends" to begin with. Trends give names to abstract developments and give us a sense of control. Many trends, however, are merely linear extrapolations of things we see today. The future may instead be shaped by phe-nomena, technological or other-wise, that seemingly come out of nowhere and explode within a few years. This kind of non-linear thinking is highly difficult to master, which leaves most of us blind to the kinds of trend that follow this sort of trajectory.

> Trends give names to abstract developments and give us a sense of control

5. *Invisibility by presentism – We believe that tomorrow will be like today, more or less.*
   Henry Ford famously said that people would most likely have wanted "faster horses" had he asked them what he could produce for them. Similarly, we often fail to take many changes into account because they challenge our worldview too much. We like to think that the future is somewhat familiar and this sense of familiarity is what many science fiction films and television series exploit. Sure, there are fancy new gadgets and flying saucers, but the basic sociological structures in society are still intact. We want to think that only the leaves on the tree will change and not the tree's stem and branches.

6. *Invisibility by myopia – We believe that our world is the world.*

   We all believe that the image of the world we see before our eyes is an accurate portrayal of the world as it really is. If this silent agreement between eyes and brain were to be broken, we would most likely succumb to madness. Human consciousness is a lot more complex than this, however, and the world we see when we peer out is a highly personal one. This means that most people have their own little trend map, and when a critical mass of people register a certain phenomenon, that's when we start referring to it as "a trend", "a fad" or "the new, new thing", even if it has been with us for several years.

7. *Invisibility by pessimism – Since we are all doomed, how can things get better?*

   People are sloppy when thinking about the future. We spend 12 per cent of our time – an hour of every eight-hour working day – thinking about the future, but few of us use this hour constructively. We tend to quickly ponder certain questions – most of them negative – only to let them slide into oblivion as quickly as they arose. Will I get promoted? Will my children be happy? What if I fall ill? When will the markets crash? When will the next terrorist strike happen? And so on. These are questions that tend to make us worry. The result is that our overall vision of the future is one of gloom and doom. Most media channels do their part to add to this drama as well.

   **We are loss-averse and tend to fear and grieve loss more than we celebrate winning**

   Have you ever read a newspaper focusing on happy news? Of course not. News thrives on drama, conflict, pain, misery and destruction that we can relate to. Furthermore, we are loss-averse and tend to fear and grieve loss more than we celebrate winning. All this adds up to a collective vision of the future as quite a bleak place. What we miss because of this is all the ways in which the world is becoming a better place. A healthier, happier, wealthier, more peaceful place.

Each chapter will be followed by a Trendspotter Mission Manual, in which I will inspire you to apply the ideas I've just raised to become a better trendspotter. The missions I've laid out are intended to be short, simple and potentially mind-altering. I want to promote better trendspotting and future thinking by making you aware of these seven trendspotting pitfalls. These errors of vision and perception stem from deeply rooted psychological mechanisms, so attempting to cure them completely is too big a challenge. We'll leave that to the "Change your life in seven days" writers. Yet I believe that making people aware of these shortcomings represents a first step towards a world where more people have a truer worldview – not always more optimistic, but more useful. To make decisions. To make more money. To make us happier as human beings. Let's go trendspotting!

# 1 Blinded by slow motion

## How mass entrepreneurship is redefining capitalism ... slowly

*I wonder if I've been changed in the night? Let me think: was I the same when I got up this morning? I almost think I can remember feeling a little different. But if I'm not the same, the next question is "Who in the world am I?" Ah, that's the great puzzle!*

– Lewis Carroll, *Alice's Adventures in Wonderland*

## Lost in time

Why do we find closed communities – the Amish, African tribes, South American Indians, Buddhist monks, and so on – so fascinating? I believe that the main reason is that we perceive these groups as static, in stark contrast to the dynamic, chaotic life we live in an increasingly urban, globalized world. We change. They don't. This, however, is a half-truth. We might change as a group over time but not necessarily as individuals. Think about the number of times you've heard racist or sexist jokes made by someone who has grown up in another era. Think about all the distinguished gentlemen who insist on using historical battles to describe events in modern business. Think about the number of times you've heard that "they don't make *real* music or movies any more". All these are symptoms of frozen minds that have failed to adapt to a changing society. We all learned about the world we live in at a certain stage in our life and unlearning this knowledge is very hard. This chapter will look at why we find it so hard to update our mental models to a new world, and it will also give an example of a veritable revolution – or at least a revolutionary evolution – that has taken place in the past decades.

## Loving to hate capitalism

Few words and concepts are as polarizing and certain to stir up debate as "capitalism". Defenders tend to dogmatically defend it and accuse others of not understanding "what capitalism is *really* about". Attackers claim to have seen through capitalism as if it were an illusion. Don't get me wrong. I'm well aware that, unless we live in Cuba or North Korea, we *are* capitalists. We pay for our homes, usually get paid in accordance with our efforts or ideas and tend to pay others for the goods and services that we want to consume. Many of us, however, can be classified as reluctant capitalists and subscribe to the popular view that "capitalism is the least bad economic system yet invented". The flaws, whether caused by capitalism or merely by-products of it, make themselves apparent every once in a while. The global financial crisis in the autumn of 2008 made it fashionable to talk about the "Death of Capitalism". Even before this, media reports often focused on the "other side" of capitalism, from inhumane treatment of labourers in emerging economies to CEOs who had embezzled, lied or cheated. To determine whether the problems are actually caused by capitalism or by the flaws inherent in any society is beside the point. Many people *perceive* these problems to be caused by capitalism and therefore tend to feel that its image is tainted and that there must be a better alternative looming somewhere ahead of us. Capitalism is a system used, even accepted, by almost everyone but loved by few. Why?

## ● Crabgrass or elfgrass?

In an episode of *The Simpsons*, Homer made the claim that the only reason people dislike crabgrass is because of its name. If we had called it "elfgrass", it wouldn't be seen as a problem, was his argument. Capitalism suffers from something similar. The very word implies that the world should revolve around capital, not people. The consequence is that many things that are of tremendous value to human beings – love, dreams, hopes and fears – tend to be either disregarded by capitalism or misshapen by it – paying for love is known as prostitution, to use an example. What if we were to call the system by which economic society operates "humanism"? The concept would remain largely the same but the word would gain in semantic attractiveness, and perhaps make "the system formerly known as capitalism" more popular. Then again, superficial branding exercises like this tend to disregard the root causes of problems. Studying anti-capitalist literature, it soon becomes apparent that what people tend to dislike is how the system itself operates, not just its name. Frequently occurring causes of complaint include the rise of megacorporations and the decline of civic society, the loss of labour rights, the loss of citizenry, monopolization, a disregard of the poor and the have-nots, and so on. In fact, many people even criticize capitalism for being an "ism", since it implies that capitalism is an idea thrust upon people that they have to believe in, assimilate to and work as subordinates for – just like communism or fascism.

Many critics, however, fail to see that what we call capitalism today is entirely different from the capitalism of yesterday. Capitalism has changed in the past decades. Its changes, however, have been slow and gradual, and when changes are slow, they tend to become invisible. Slow and gradual changes are unable to compete with the plethora of sudden and sensational messages that reach us on a daily basis. The media's relentless focus on terrorist strikes, stock market falls, corporate scandals and the injustice suffered by the less fortunate blind us to what's happening on a deeper, slower level. This chapter will discuss this concept of gradual change and how gradualism has transformed capitalism into something new without many of us noticing.

**When changes are slow, they tend to become invisible**

## ● The twelve-second rule

The human brain is highly efficient at detecting change. Introduce a new odour into a room, plant a penguin in a sea of white doves or try to persuade people that a computer-animated person is real and virtually everyone will see the discrepancies, or, at least,

**The human brain is highly efficient at detecting change**

will claim "something isn't quite right". On another level, though, people are blind to change. The most effective way of concealing it is to make it slower, more gradual and less drastic. If the penguin is slowly and gradually introduced into an image of white doves or the strength of the new odour is slowly and gradually increased, most people will be unable to detect it. Experiments in human perception have shown that the limit between perceiving something and being oblivious to it can be drawn at twelve seconds. In images where a rock slowly appears in a river or an object changes colour or a building appears, people are unable to see anything but a static image if the changes take twelve seconds or longer to appear. Imagine how invisible this renders changes that take place over years, even decades. Slow change is why science fiction movies are so efficient, since they catapult the viewer into a futuristic world where everything would actually seem quite normal if we had been given some decades to adapt. Major changes often come stealthily like this. Their revolutionary effects may reside in the fact that we do not recognize what they are doing to our behaviour and our way of thinking, and so we cannot resist them.[1]

## ● Our frozen minds

My grandmother lives alone in a suburb of Stockholm. When I visit her – which isn't as often as it should be – I have thought about how old-fashioned her interior style is. From the murky colour schemes to the antique furniture. This is something I used to fear when I was younger. When will "old-person taste" set in? I somehow envisioned a certain age when all the cool gadgets and furniture that I owned would be replaced by the stale stuff that filled my grandmother's flat. Now I realize that her apartment is a perfect real-world representation of the human mind. When we grow up, our minds are fluid and open to new learning and impressions, but slowly, over time, our minds freeze up and we settle in our ways and perspectives. Some views and values even harden into dogma. Like most people, my grandmother developed her aesthetic taste and bought most of her furniture before she was fifty. The stuff that fills her apartment was high fashion when she bought it. She's as hip as she's ever been, but time has passed and taste has moved on. The same thing will most likely happen to me. My minimalist, Scandinavian-design furniture, which I consider "timeless", will be viewed as stale old-person antiques when I'm in my eighties. The same thing goes for my taste in music and movies, as well as most of my views and opinions. If you don't stop and look around you every once in a while, your brain will become like an old person's apartment.

## Capitalism redefined

When you add these two phenomena together – invisible gradual change and frozen minds – you have a cocktail for misunderstanding and one of the main causes of inter-generational friction. Television, computer games, the rise of Asia, gay marriage, anal sex, racist jokes and rock music are just some of the areas of conflict stemming from the fact that different generations have grown up in different societies with value systems and preferences that have slowly changed over time. So how does capitalism fit into this conflict?

Go back a century or two and the kind of capitalism we lived with was characterized by near anarchy. Robber barons, weak institutions, non-existent business legislation, few labour rights and stale, monopolized markets. These are claims that anti-capitalists still use to oppose this system. In the decades following the Second World War, however, capitalism began to change in a way that would transform it completely. The change has been slow and gradual, rendering it invisible to most people, yet we are confronted with the effects of it on a daily basis. This change is called individualization, the force whereby the individual – not the group – has become more powerful than ever in the history of civilization.

## ● From "Is it possible?" to "Do I want to?"

I hated business school. For me, it had been a compromise between what I wanted to do in life and what I felt I should do. The latter side won and off to business school I went. After three years of debits, credits, formulas and pink newspapers, I needed a break. I decided to try out my real passion, film-making. I applied to a local film school in Stockholm and got in. I envisioned myself as a wunderkind who would soon be discovered and leave the grey business world for the glamour of Hollywood. Boy, was I wrong. Film school turned out to be an institution even more conservative than the Stockholm School of Economics, where I studied business. We spent endless sessions watching incomprehensible French movies that our professors wanted us to admire. The afternoons were spent learning the tools of production, something that entailed fiddling around with a video camera or staring admiringly at a real 35mm Arriflex film camera. This was an important distinction. Video was a tool for amateurs doing amateur stuff. The Arriflex was a *real* film camera, just as French *nouvelle vague* films were examples of *real* movie-making. The barriers to making a *real* film were high and numerous. Many budding film-makers were called. Very few were chosen. The question we anxiously asked ourselves while admiring the Arriflex or dozing off to the works of Godard, Truffaut et al. was: "Is it possible? Will I ever be chosen to make a movie?"

Fast-forward a decade and a decent video camera is now available for free in every new mobile phone. Editing software is available online for free. More importantly, global film distribution – previously one of the highest barriers of entry to the film market – is free. In this world, the question we ask is not whether it is possible to make a movie but "Do I want to make a movie?" Ten years ago, many of us could hide our artistic ineptitude behind complaints about the impenetrability of the system. Today, we have fewer excuses. Technology has created a world where everyone can make a movie. Most of these films don't compete in the arena of big blockbusters but have created their own arena, where the rules are different. In fact, there are no rules. Virtually anything can be characterized as a movie. Three minutes of a laughing baby. A guy dressed up as Jesus dancing to "I Will Survive". A sneezing panda. And so on. Some mock and ridicule this development and still refer to French *nouvelle vague* fare as *real* films. That is missing the point entirely. We stand at the beginning of an era where the individual is given the tools that were once only given to qualified, chosen professionals. The individual becomes self-confident and adds his or her vision to a field that was previously open only to the interpretations of very few people, mostly middle-aged men. They dictated what was made. They dictated what qualified as *right* or *wrong*. And guess what? Film-making is only one of many examples of this power shift.

**Technology has created a world where everyone can make a movie**

## Why 9/11 makes me optimistic

I quit my job as a brand strategy consultant on 10 September 2001. I was gathering up stuff at my office desk the next day when someone told us to come into to the conference room and watch TV. Seeing the tragedies unfold on live TV made me terrified, saddened, outraged and all the other adjectives that we've come across so many times in the years since the terrorist attacks. The stock market needed only a few weeks to rebound. The human mind took a lot longer. When I gained some perspective, I realized that amid all the chaos, sadness, destruction and pure evil that these attacks represented was one thought to be somewhat optimistic about: the attacks were the result of just nineteen guys. Earlier acts of war had needed thousands of soldiers backed by entire nations. These nineteen hijackers were indeed backed by a network of like-minded people but the direct cost, in cash, for the operation was negligible, so they could have acted without the help of al-Qaeda if they had wanted to. Nineteen guys. A world turned upside down. Fewer can do more, a fact that sadly includes deeds of destruction as well as ones of creativity. With this thought in mind, I started to look around at the clients I worked with and at what was happening in their industries.

Fewer can do more

## ● The army of me

Being small used to be an excuse. "We're just a small company," we would say, and use it as a reason for not going global, not making investments, not creating change and so on. These days, small has become an advantage. Making a fashion range used to be a very expensive endeavour. You needed to have access to a factory, capital and labour. These days, you need a phone number for one of the many production consultants whose networks span the facilities in Europe and Asia. I saw this first hand when I worked with a fashion company in the sports and leisure industry. They used to have a handful of competitors who they knew by name and could second-guess when each new season began. These days, they are swarmed by a myriad of competitors. Some guy from Alaska has created a cool range of jackets. An Asian upstart has this year's hottest ski pants. And so on. Here today and gone tomorrow. Only to be replaced by even smaller, stranger and more unpredictable competition. As barriers to enter the market have come down, the number of competitors, real and perceived, has shot up. The financial industry is starting to look much the same even though it is subject to much stricter regulation. Working with a large bank, I realized that the financial playing field was being drastically redrawn. At one end were the big, merged conglomerates, but at the other end was a tsunami of small upstarts, individual investors, shareholder activists, day traders and hackers who programmed everything from algorithms to bots that would mimic hedge funds. The story continues and appears much the same wherever I've looked. Sports equipment, consumer durables, travel and transport, technology, IT, and so on. Even politics is being characterized by large, established parties on the one hand – often more polarized than ever – and a plethora of grassroots movements and political entrepreneurs on the other. All over the world, individuals – acting alone or in groups – are making a bigger impact than ever before. The tools for creation, distribution and, most importantly, discovery have been spread among the masses. We are all creators, distributors and trendspotters.

**The tools for creation, distribution and discovery have been spread among the masses**

## ● Liberating the individual

Technology is the most apparent liberator of individuals, but technology never exists in a vacuum. It is shaped and honed by the people who use it. Another factor contributing to individualization is the attitude shift away from collectivism and towards individualism. Collectivism is the idea that society exists for groups while the desires and needs of separate individuals are inferior to those of the collective. Conversely, individualism is the idea that society is made up of separate individuals whose needs and desires should always prevail in a group, with the added disclaimer "as long as it doesn't harm other people". Societies around the world were far more collectivist in the early 1900s than they are now. Clergy, kings, emperors and classes were more prevalent and powerful than they are today. What happened? Two world wars is what. The First World War, or the Great War as it was known then, killed the idea that politicians were benign rulers who put the interests of their people first. The Great War was different since most of the opposing parties depended, at least to start with, on volunteers and it was, in many but not all cases, fought by democracies. All of a sudden, politicians needed to plead with and court public opinion. Soldiers were enlisted by use of – often false – propaganda. The machine gun and other "killer applications", in the true sense of the word, enabled battlefield slaughter on a whole new level. The result of these changes was a massive hangover and widespread disillusionment with the powers that be. The Church was swept along on this wave of doubt. How can there be a God if there is killing on this scale? The idea that politicians lie and the loosened grip of faith are themes that echo to this day.

Just over two decades later, another blow was dealt to collectivism. The Second World War showed us what happens when one nation succumbs to the ideas of a single ruler. Nazism was collectivism gone very, very bad. It is no coincidence that the decades following 1945 gave rise to the rebel, the beatnik, the hippy, rock music and other counterculture ideas. The choice was either to break free of society's shackles or perish. Nations that hadn't been close to the wars were still affected by the forces of fashion – it became hip to be unique, to throw away all ideas of a uniform and follow your own path instead. The technological revolution that brought us the World Wide Web and mobile-phone cameras was only the most recent development in a trend that occurred for the greater part of the twentieth century.

Only recently, however, has this change in attitude been reflected in economic terms.

## Earning money or making money

The *World Wealth Report* is a study of the world's rich. Published annually, it focuses on the numbers, net worth and investment strategies of people who have far more money than you or me. The 2003 edition contained a diagram[2] that fundamentally changed my worldview.

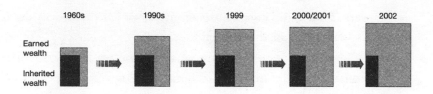

On the left-hand side, we see what the rich were like up to and including the 1960s. The money was predominantly inherited – acquired by being the heir to family wealth. Back then, borrowing money was cumbersome, regulated and expensive. Getting money if you were not lucky enough to be born rich or marry a millionaire came down to either working for some sort of family firm, stealing or winning the lottery. This society frowned upon risk. Squandering hard-earned family heirlooms on frivolous and risky projects was very rare. Movement between income brackets was slow, if it occurred at all.

Taking the time machine to the present, fifty years on, we see a world where wealth is primarily self-made. More than two-thirds of the world's billionaires acquired their own wealth without inheriting a single penny.[3] Self-made. Created. Something out of nothing. As a Swede, I envy the English, who have a word for

**Today, we can do *whatever* we want**

this. To *make* money. In Sweden, we say only "*tjäna pengar*" – earn money, implying that we are dependent on someone else to give it to us as a reward. Borrowing money has become cheap and accessible. Perhaps too cheap and accessible if we consider the resulting credit crunch. Readily accessible funds, however, have created a world where we're no longer limited to marrying rich people or robbing banks if we want money. Today, we can do *whatever we want*. Tie a piece of rubber around someone's foot, push him or her off a cliff, call it bungee jumping and charge money for the effort. Fantasize about a boy wizard at a boarding school. Write Java code. Create a better algorithm. Write a song about sex. Sell a better burger. Whatever we want. Like being kids whose parents have left them with the house to themselves for the weekend.

Making money by doing whatever we want creates a level of freedom that is almost unimaginable. Slowly, people are realizing this. The number of people who claim that their ultimate dream is to start their own company has been increasing drastically around the world in the past decade. When interviewing young people of various nationalities a few years ago, I was struck by how similar people's answers were when I asked them what they envisioned themselves doing professionally in ten years' time. "I will be running my own company" was the ubiquitous answer, whether we were in Bogotá, Birmingham or Borås. In the United States, more than five thousand entrepreneurship programmes are offered on two- and four-year courses – up from just 250 in 1985. Full-scale majors, minors or certificates in entrepreneurship have leaped from 104 in 1975 to more than 500 in 2006.[4] With large companies laying people off or going bankrupt, these numbers will only increase. Why trust someone else for employment and work for somebody else's goals and dreams? This is what happened in Japan during the recession of the 1990s , the so-called "Lost Decade":

> Recession [boosted Japan's young creatives], discrediting Japan's
> rigid social hierarchy and empowering young entrepreneurs. It
> may also have loosened the grip a big-business career track had
> over so much of Japan's workforce, who now face fewer social
> stigmas for experimenting with art, music, or any number of
> similar, risky endeavours ... "There's a new creativeness [in
> Japan] because there's less money."[5]

## ● The challenger society

We have moved from a top-down society – "do as you're told" – to a bottom-up one, where people want to challenge and change society.

We can call people growing up in this climate "Generation E", where E stands for entrepreneurship. Today's students have heard more about Bill Gates and Google than about Winston Churchill or FDR. Entrepreneurship doesn't just mean "starting your own company". It describes an entire attitude that I liken to punk rock. Punk was built on two ideas. The first was that it wanted to change the world. It was an angry music genre. Anarchy in the UK. Challenge the status quo. This is the modus operandi for entrepreneurs. A cheaper airline. A better song. A nicer bed. A friendlier staff. And so on. The second idea of punk rock – and the reason it sometimes sounded appalling – was that it was built around the notion that anyone can play. Skill is oppression. Anyone can hammer away on drums, scream into a microphone or strum on a guitar. Individualization creates a world where anyone can play, make a video, create a gadget, program a computer, write a blog, design a jacket. It isn't so strange that Bono, lead singer of U2, termed the current economic climate "punk capitalism".

> Individualization creates a world where anyone can play, make a video, create a gadget

## New wine in new bottles

If you were an entrepreneur before the rise of the World Wide Web, you tended to copy and create better versions of something local. Something that already existed. A better newspaper. A better bank. A better shoe shop. And so on. I remember attending a government-financed "Start your own company" seminar in Stockholm in 1994. One of the organizers – a corpulent civil servant in a greyish suit – took to the stage to inspire us. "What if you started your own bookkeeping firm?" he mused. "Or your own garage?" These were the kinds of ideas that sprang to mind when people thought about "starting my own company" in 1994. Some entrepreneurs had the funds available to travel far away and bring something back that people hadn't seen before, but there were not many of them.

The Web has made this rarity a mainstream phenomenon. Discovering Indian shoe shops, American pizza parlours, Chinese MP3 players, Dutch vending machines and other business ideas has become as easy as opening up a newspaper. This creates an environment where new business ideas tend to be more revolutionary than ever before. How so? The unanimous verdict among creativity experts is that new ideas are merely combinations of old ones. In a world without an Internet, most ideas that we could see, touch and understand were local. Today, we can see examples of offerings, technologies and products from virtually any industry around the world at the click of a mouse button. We can study scientific papers, read academic journals or learn computer programming. The possibilities are endless, and so are the number of new combinations we can make between all these existing ideas. Think about some of the most revolutionary business innovations of the past decade. They are not just clones of something that existed elsewhere. They are pioneers. Imagine someone imagining Google before the advent of the Web. Fifty people sitting in a warehouse armed with telephones answering people's queries. Slow, cumbersome and expensive. The Web has turbocharged innovative thinking by exposing more people to more ideas in an easy, inexpensive way.

> New ideas are merely combinations of old ones

## ● How to be unique

When I attended business school, the student union sent a mocking note to all newly enrolled students. It said: "Who do you think you are? The CEO of Volvo Cars? The minister of finance? ... Nope, you're just a silly first-year student ..." A silly student. Not the CEO of Sweden's most admired company. Or a hotshot politician. The world used to be about this kind of hierarchy. The more you differed, in terms of age, gender, skin colour, education and experience, from the governing classes, the worse off you were. Nowadays, original thinkers capable of creating original products and services are the people driving the economy. The most interesting entrepreneurial ideas may occasionally be launched by large, established companies, but more often they will be found at the fringes of society. From the misfits, the young, the strange, the quirky and the nerdy. In a world of inherited wealth, it was all about management. Managing wealth. Managing companies. Preserving values. Not rocking the boat too much. A formal, hierarchically based education system was the basic building block of that society. People were cogs that fitted into a well-oiled machine.

**Risk-taking, creativity and imagination have become the most important skills or traits**

Nowadays, when wealth is self-made, risk-taking, creativity and imagination have become the most important skills or traits. Skin colour, formal education, gender, age and surname matter less than ever. Becoming a millionaire is more democratic than it was. Not easier, but more democratic. Yesterday's educational system was focused upon creating clones and putting everyone through the same one-size-fits-all system. Today's education should be about embracing uniqueness, fostering independent and creative thinking, as well as teaching people to take risks. You can't learn to be unique. You can only embrace your own uniqueness or destroy it.

**You can't learn to be unique**

## ● Old school versus new school

I learned how to ski downhill when I was a young boy in the early 1980s. Like all other kinds of education, learning then flowed from top to bottom. Older ski instructors told us how to ski the *right* way. Knees slightly bent and separated by the width of an imagined toilet roll. Put the poles in the ground as you turned. Favour the outside ski. And so on. I learned how to ski really well. In 2005, I was skiing in Norway when a teenager remarked that I had a really cool "old-school French style" when I skied. Old. School. French. Style. I was mortified. I am young. I ski well. It turned out that skiing had slowly, gradually been transformed into something else. Now, you can ski however you want to. Monkey stance. Jib, rail, half-pipe. Do big air jumps that you name after yourself. Do it your way. The punk way. When the model of teaching is shifted from top-down and allowed instead to emerge from below, the playing field is broadened, the barriers come down and the sport is enriched. Growth in downhill skiing was stagnant for two decades until this "new-school skiing" flourished. Now, it's a growing sport again.

## ● Standard becomes personal

As a futurologist – a more pretentious description of my profession – I sometimes think about what traits and phenomena, prevalent today, will be mocked and ridiculed by tomorrow's generations. The one thing that most often crosses my mind is the idea of standardization – the one-size-fits-all model of production that fuelled much of the growth in the twentieth century. Before the advent of mass production, few things looked or sounded the same. Music always differed because it was always played live. Stories were passed on between generations, each one of which added and took away parts of the story to remix them into something new. Products were handmade and differed in quality, taste, looks and feel. Standardization brought prices down and enabled more people to afford music, books, cars, food and other necessities. It also eliminated the kind of uniqueness that characterizes individuals.

Today, thanks to technological development, personalization is returning. People can mould and create their own products and services. From tailoring your own news flow by RSS – something every

trendspotter should be doing – stitching together your own TV schedule with digital recorders and designing your own shirt online to 3D printers that enable

**Standardization is the anomaly. Personalization is the natural state**

people to sculpt and model products with a market of only one person – themselves. Personalization is more in sync with human nature. No individual's needs are exactly identical to somebody else's. Standardization is the anomaly. Personalization is the natural state.

## ● Doing it for love

On a recent walk in one of Stockholm's suburbs, I came across a little paper note stapled to a tree. "Lost gloves found. Please call this number if they're yours", it said, with a name and phone number written below. Somebody had found a pair of gloves and made the effort to go home, sit down and write a paper note, slide it into a plastic folder and then go back to where the gloves were found and staple it to a nearby tree using a stapler that they had also brought with them from home. Since we were in a park, the nearest house was a good five minutes away. Imagining, perhaps wrongly, that this person lived in the nearest house, I calculated that this person had just spent at least thirty minutes on helping a complete stranger.

Besides being a case for optimism (or a bad conscience for those of us who wouldn't have devoted thirty minutes to finding the rightful owners of lost gloves), the example illustrates a hidden economy at work. I'm not referring to the grey sector of the economy, which is made up of people paying each other under the table without the tax authorities being notified. This hidden economy is made up of all the areas in life and society where people do each other favours: retrieve lost gloves or wallets, fiddle around with their hobbies, make a cake or a drawing for a loved one, edit a home movie to show friends, and so on. These are activities that people spend a lot of time doing but don't consider economic activities. We don't view baking a cake or making a mix tape as either "work" or "a cost". They are simply things we do because we want to. Because we like to. Amateur has come to denote work that is done without getting paid and from which we shouldn't expect the

**Amateur, however, has the same stem as the word *amore* – meaning love**

same high quality that denotes ("real") professional work. Amateur, however, has the same etymological stem as the word *amore* – meaning love. What we should consider is that there are two different economies; one is the formal, professional, transaction-based economy that we think about when we hear the word "economy". The other is a hidden, invisible economy, where the currency is time and love with some loose change thrown in for good measure.

This secret economy matters because whereas these "glove retrievers" are quite few in number, they can easily get in touch on the Internet. There may even be a number of Glove Retriever communities where people who like finding the rightful owners of lost property can share advice and stories. In a non-connected world, everybody went at it alone. The person who retrieved the glove may also be a Kiss fan or enjoy *Surströmming* (fermented, rotten fish – a Swedish "delicacy"). He or she can now easily find many other like-minded people around the world when, only a decade or so ago, they were doomed to an isolated suburban existence, where few understood their taste in fish or music, let alone the half-hour sacrificed for a complete stranger. The world is becoming a warmer place. Not just through climate change but through more quirky people finding other people with the same quirks. Blessed are the freaks and the geeks, for they shall inherit the earth.

# "... ism"

Perhaps the most damning feature of capitalism is the fact that it's an "ism", denoting that it's a complete ready-to-wear, from-above philosophy and mindset. When something becomes an "ism", it's viewed as dogmatic, rigid and polarizing in a "you're-either-with-us-or-against-us" kind of way. Fascism, communism and capitalism are worlds apart in their basic assumptions and ways of working, but on a superficial level they sound similar. This may be yet another reason why people so vehemently oppose it. Not just because they perceive it to be unfair and insensitive but also because the very idea of an "ism" governing a society is out of touch with the human mindset.

What we can see happening now is that the "ism" part of capitalism is disappearing. Power, influence and knowledge used to flow one way from above and trickle down in the hierarchy. Now, they're growing from below. The individual becomes powerful. The individual can make money. Capitalism has been transformed into something we can call MyCapital. It's your capital. You decide how to make it and what to do with it. MyCapital is a microcosm. How I made money and what I want to do with it might have very little to do with the capital that you have acquired. Millionaires used to be viewed as exploiters. MyCapital

**These days, millionaires come in all shapes and colours**

millionaires make an effort to give back. They formulate and pursue audacious goals. Terminate malaria. Wipe out poverty. Create a better fuel. Go green. Being a millionaire used to mean being a corpulent gentleman in a suit. These days, millionaires come in all shapes and colours. Female, black, slim, athletic, strange, a punk rocker, a misfit, young or old. In a world of self-made wealth, anyone can do it. MyCapital is the individualistic version of capitalism that enables you to trim away any parts of the "ism" that you don't like.

## ● Next

When the financial crisis hit the world with full force in the autumn of 2008, it became fashionable for magazine covers and editorials to proclaim "The Death of Capitalism". Alas, they were right. But capitalism isn't dying the quick and dramatic death we could follow in the news headlines. It's slowly fading away to be replaced by a new version. This evolved version, MyCapital, is more personal, less rigid and places the individual in the driver's seat.

The new version may still seem hazy to many people. After all, we are groomed to view the world in terms of big companies, big employers and "regular" jobs. Isn't that the world most people live in? Not true. Think about the number of professions today that didn't exist in the mid-1990s. Flash programmers. Trendspotters. Citizen journalists. Information designers. MySpace celebrities. Bloggers. And so on. These are self-made professions that spontaneously emerged when the world changed. They were not invented in the R&D department of a multinational or dreamt up by parents or politicians. MyCapital will continue to unfold its wings in the coming years. Like a giant Swiss Army knife, it will show new features and tools. Some of them will be unpleasant. Nineteen guys with the wrong idea about paradise can wreak havoc on an entire world. Most of MyCapital's features, however, will improve our world. What happens when the individual can manipulate atoms and genes the same way we manipulate snippets of information, zeros and ones, today? What happens when flying long haul becomes as cheap as flying shorter trips? What happens when even more people from around the world can connect to share ideas and experiences? Our imagination, not elderly men with fancy surnames, will give us the answers.

## ● Gradually then suddenly

Capitalism has slowly been redefined in the past decades and this slow, gradual change is invisible. This means that anyone who made their mind up about the way the world works a few decades ago is bound to hold on to those opinions regardless of how many entrepreneurial upstarts he or she comes across. Values and perspectives tend to harden into blinding dogma if they're not continually updated. "Continual updating" is a cumbersome way of describing what happens when people are curious and ask themselves "what if?" every now and then. That is the simple cure for this particular kind of blindness. If my grandmother had made a point of completely refurnishing her apartment every few years, she wouldn't have the old-fashioned style she has now. If you and I continually refurnish our minds every few years – change reading habits, make an effort to talk to new people or travel to different places – chances are that we will be able to detect these slow-moving "turtle trends" before they surprise us. And surprise us they will. Like a heart attack, these trends tend to slowly unfold under the radar for decades before making their big, noisy and sometimes unpleasant debut on the world stage.

**Values and perspectives tend to harden into blinding dogma if they're not continually updated**

9/11 is just one of many examples of a world taken by surprise by a new world order that had been developing for decades. September 2008 taught the world a lesson about increased complexities and interdependences that had been created over decades. Big companies fail to attract new talent because they all want to "do their own thing". Taking a long view of events is something of an immunization against unexpected events. Had we considered stock market performance and growth figures during the entire twentieth century – not just assumed that the miraculous years between 1987 and 2007 were the norm – financial meltdowns and stock market busts would have come as no surprise.

The next chapter will focus on what happens when the playing field is reshuffled, and why we often fail to see these reshufflings happening.

# The Trendspotter Mission Manual

Determined to upgrade your mental maps and models of the world?
Good! Here are a number of things you can do

**DON'T LIVE IN THE PRESENT!**
IGNORE ALL THE WONKY ADVICE GIVEN BY SELF-HELP GURUS AND NEW AGE COLUMNISTS. YOU NEED TO FOCUS ON THE DISTANT PAST AND THE FUTURE. THERE ARE A NUMBER OF WAYS IN WHICH TO DO THIS.

**VISIT YOUR GRANDMOTHER!**
OR ANY ELDERLY PERSON FOR THAT MATTER. TALK TO THEM ABOUT WHAT IT WAS LIKE TO LIVE A LONG TIME AGO. TAKE NOTES AND LOOK FOR ANOMALIES. WHAT WAS DIFFERENT THEN AND WHAT MIGHT THIS TELL US ABOUT HOW THE WORLD HAS CHANGED?

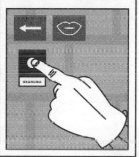

**DEDRAMATIZE!**
STAY AWAY FROM THE HYPERBOLIC LANGUAGE PEOPLE USE TO DESCRIBE PRESENT, SHORT-TERM THINGS LIKE NEW ELECTRONIC GADGETS OR SENSATIONAL NEWS. THIS LANGUAGE SHOULD BE RESERVED FOR GROUNDBREAKING REVOLUTIONS SUCH AS THE LONG-TERM CHANGE OF CAPITALISM, FOR EXAMPLE.

**LOVE YOUR LIBRARY! SCREW THE NEWSSTAND!**
LIBRARIES ARE WHERE WE CAN FIND PERSPECTIVE. READ HISTORY BOOKS, STUDY HISTORICAL PORTRAITS OF YOUR CITY, STUDY OLD MAPS.

**FIND PROGRESSIONS!**
THE BEST KIND OF STATISTICS ARE THE ONES THAT SHOW PROGRESSIONS OVER TIME. GET THE LONG VIEW OF STOCK MARKET PERFORMANCE OR "NUMBER OF HOURS WORKED."

**CHANGE YOUR MEDIA HABITS!**
THINK OF YOURSELF AS IF YOU'RE ON A DIET REGIMEN. YOU NEED TO FEED YOUR HEAD WITH NEW INPUT, SO DEFINE A NUMBER OF NEW SOURCES MAGAZINES, BLOGS, BOOKS AND PEOPLE THAT WILL GIVE YOU NEW PERSPECTIVES.

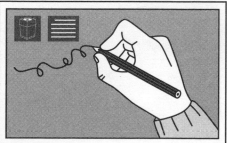

**TAKE NOTES!**
GATHER YOUR THOUGHTS ABOUT WHAT YOU SEE, NO MATTER HOW FRAGMENTED THEY ARE. BE AN OPPORTUNISTIC COLLECTOR OF FACTS, IDEAS, QUOTES, PICTURES AND THOUGHTS.

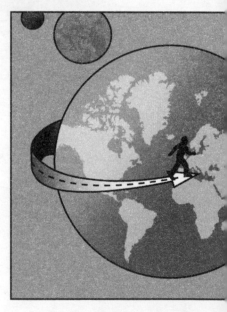

# 2 Seeing through the matrix

## How the illusion of boundaries and borders is crumbling

*Blinding ignorance does mislead us. O! Wretched mortals, open your eyes!*

– Leonardo da Vinci

## ● Night on earth

Looking at the dark half of earth in photographs taken from space, something striking becomes clear: nations are a myth. The lights shining in certain places at night show no respect for man-made borders drawn in the sand. Just like ideas, capital, communication, goods and people, they keep shining across nations and regions. A wonderful portrait of the boundarylessness of mankind.

It's easy to assume that nations are natural. This is the view taught in many schools. We are Sweden, China or Mongolia, and we always intended to be. Listening to lyrics of national anthems, it's easy to be misled into thinking that nations are God-given and an inevitable fate of all people. The nation, however, is a man-made innovation, and just as vinyl records and freon refrigerators have been replaced by modern alternatives, the nation-state is approaching its sell-by date. This chapter will focus on why we are prone to view things in terms of fixed borders and how the national and market-drawn boundaries are currently being redrawn or eliminated completely.

**The nation-state is approaching its sell-by date**

## ● Things fall apart

What if your mind had to start from the beginning every morning when you woke up? What if nothing you've ever learned stuck and you had to spend each day trying to establish the patterns, rules, laws and relationships that the majority of us live with? You would have to determine whether the person sleeping next to you was your wife. You would be surprised that things fell downward. You would marvel at the unique consistency and colour of water. You would approach each person you met on the street with a sense of awe and wonder.

To many of us, this would be the very definition of hell; a place where everything that makes life worth living – love, memories, knowledge – would be obsolete. To others, this naive way of approaching life and learning may have its charms, but these people would probably prefer to choose when to switch this ability on and off. Human consciousness is a mystery, but something we do know is that the human mind creates rules and regulations so we don't have to wake up every day and rediscover the world completely. *This is my wife. There is gravity. I am a man.* And so on. But how many of these assumptions and rules are illusions? Mental constructions made for convenience rather than accuracy? What if many of the things we "know" are wrong? What happens when the lens that we see the world through becomes outdated?

## ● Solid comfort

Why do we refer to the spherical planet on which we live as "Earth"? Why do we let a single coin symbolize an entire country's monetary policy when we say "the Swedish krona" or "the British pound"? Why do we let a single colour symbolize all things that are environmentally friendly or an erroneous skin colour description – "white" – symbolize Caucasians? These are examples of metonymies – letting small things symbolize bigger concepts. The reason this and other types of metaphors are so useful is that the human mind is poorly built for complexity. We saw in the previous chapter that the human mind is blind to changes that take place over longer periods of time. Similarly, we are blind to

**We are blind to happenings that are too small to detect with the naked eye**

happenings that are too big in scope or too small to detect with the naked eye. Human beings tend to focus on and understand the things that take place before their eyes and alter anything outside this limited field of vision to fit into this perspective. "Millions starving" means very little to most people since the number is too big to fathom. A picture of one starving child tends to make more of us compassionate, however. Large numbers and microscopic movements have something in common. They are both abstract. A large number is hard to process unless it is put in the context of something tangible. Microscopic movements are only detectable through powerful microscopes. What we see at a superficial level tends to be static. Take any rock or pebble as an example. The rock is a potent symbol for the rigid, solid, trustworthy and unwavering; "We stood like a rock in the storm" is one of many examples of this view. Think about what a rock is actually made up of. Atoms, of course. Atoms that tend to spend their days in constant movement. The thought that something is as "solid as a rock" works only because on our level of vision a rock seems static and solid. In reality, it is made up of constantly moving parts.

The atom-centric view of the world can also be used as evidence for reincarnation. All New Age sceptics, of which I am one, cannot deny that the atoms that now circulate in your body could once have been a part of an animal or of Winston Churchill. Imagine how cumbersome life would be, though, if you were constantly watching atomic movements in other people or in materials. Like the drones living alongside Keanu Reeves in *The Matrix*, we are doomed to a life where what we see when we open our eyes in the morning is an illusion created by the limited vantage point of human vision.

## ● Illusionation

National borders are created by the mind, then drawn on to maps and into national constitutions. They are figments of the imagination that have been made real because our ancestors wanted them to be. A nation is a helpful metaphor because it takes several abstract concepts – geographic area, people, history, rituals and values – and expresses them in a single name with some colour coding in the flag to boot. This used to be a good idea. In a world with kings, dictators and emperors, where our only role was as servants to higher powers, the idea of a nation that made us citizens with rights was a breath of fresh air. Looking out at the world today, it's easy to get the impression that the idea of nations is thriving, with all the emerging nations waving flags, mail-bombing their opponents during conflicts (as in Georgia in 2008) and generating monuments to their own infallibility, be they new stadiums, towers, books or ranking titles.

**National borders are a thing created in the mind**

The other way of looking at it is that nations and national borders are crumbling and will inevitably fall apart or be merged into larger entities. They crumble because the delineations that act as clear dividers are outdated. Think about all the things that transcend national borders today: ideas, individuals, money, brands, art, feelings, languages, values and much more. Even nationalism transcends nations, with Swedes celebrating Swedish midsummer in Central Park, New York, every year in June. Hand in hand with this development is the reshuffling of the corporate world. Companies used to belong to an industry, and you could easily track these industries in the stock market section of any newspaper. These days, some firms are becoming so large that it's hard to put them into one single category. Large retailers are in sales, in distribution, in manufacturing, in design, in IT and in data mining. Small firms are sprouting up everywhere to specialize or create a brand-new market niche for themselves.

This crumbling and redrawing of boundaries is known as *fragmentization*, where previously known entities fall apart, regroup and transform into something new. The metaphors that were previously used by people to understand borders and boundaries become out-dated. The reason fragmentization is increasing is that many of the assumptions on which yesterday's maps and corporate landscapes were based are simply not true any more. Nations were strong when people couldn't travel or emigrate when they wanted to. This meant that many inhabitants of a certain region were unable to compare their situation – economic or political – with that of people around the world. The Internet and cheap flights have put an end to this situation. Anyone is now free to compare his or her daily newspaper, their bank's interest rates, their politicians' ideas or the quality of life that their income buys with other offerings from around the world.

In business, barriers of entry to virtually any market used to be high. Starting a business – even a local one – was subject to high investment costs. Today, most sectors are a lot less capital inten-sive than they used to be. Earlier in the book, I outlined how many industries are becoming accessible to anyone. In the industries that are seeing an influx of new entrants – big or small – it becomes harder and harder to delineate clearly where the industry starts and where it ends. These industry segments increasingly resemble nature itself. A natural habitat is about diversity and ecological collaboration, whereas many indus-tries have been about focus, refinement and standardization. It's as if the world now wants to resemble nature again. Similarly, city lights transcending national borders on our night-time map tell us that the world wants to be global. Another area where primitive biology meets the modern world is sex. Sexual intercourse is probably the best friend of fragmentization. Wherever people meet and mix, they tend to have sex with each other, and their offspring become hybrids of genetics. My children are Swedish–Bosnian hybrids in this gen-eration, and if I look back farther they are a mixture of Serbian, Bosniak, Walloon and Scandinavian origin.

**A natural habitat is about diversity and ecological collaboration**

A precondition for sex, however, is communication, and we see today how a universal lingua franca is emerging. It's called "bad English", the most commonly spoken language in the world. Someone once said that the world will eventually consist of "tourists and refugees". In reality, we can see how the world is full of shoppers. We shop for a place to live, work and thrive, whether we are asylum seekers or merely seek a warmer climate during our retirement.

## ● From order to chaos

When you start reshuffling people and redrawing boundaries, chaos ensues. A hundred nations and as many industries have been remixed into a cocktail of diaspora and thousands of micromarkets. The human mind has trouble keeping up. The simple metaphor of a nation – limited physical space and a colourful flag – was helpful to group things together, but as my old maths teacher explained when introducing us to statistics: "When you group things together, you lose information." We missed so much information by looking at the world through the lenses of nations and boundaries. My friend, let's call him Mr Y, was born in Chile and came to Sweden as a refugee in the early 1990s. He was non-Swedish at a time when populist parties catered to nationalist feelings in Sweden. Being a "refugee" was virtually tantamount to being a useless victim in the eyes of many people. Mr Y, however, was anything but. He went on to graduate from the best business school in Scandinavia and then moved to London to work in IT, and these days makes tons of money. He's a thriving business-school refugee! Furthermore, he's also a firm socialist, having seen the downside of conservatism in the Chilean revolution that ultimately made his family flee Santiago. A socialist living a capitalist life in London. Finally, Mr Y is gay. And a devout Catholic. The lens of nationalism cannot categorize Mr Y, and I see people like him all over the place. People who on a superficial level seem part of an easy-to-categorize demographic segment but have a highly varied, rich and patchy background when you scratch the surface.

People like these challenge our idea of normalcy. Normal implies being bundled somewhere in the middle of a giant bell curve. We have the outliers – the strange people like Mr Y – and we have the safe but dull crowd in the middle. Sexual orientation is an excellent illustration of this. We used to consider heterosexuality normal and any other sexual orientation to be deviating. In terms of numbers, this assumption may still be more or less accurate. By grouping people in a "heterosexual" segment, however, we lose so much information. Log on to any porn site on the Internet – for purely scientific reasons, of course – and check out the different variations of heterosexual. There are hundreds of different fetishes, preferences, turn-ons and peculiarities within the sloppy description "heterosexual". What if everyone actually deviates sexually? What if you're the only one turned on by whatever it is that turn you on?

Porn isn't the only market whose richness has been exposed by the global scope of the Internet. Music, books, pension funds and newspapers used to be quite limited when they were distributed in a physical context. Growing up in Sweden, teenagers tended to be either heavy metal fans or fans of electronic music. With the advent of MP3 technology and cheap – even free – distribution of music, this division between subgroups crumbles, with people now cramming their music players with songs from all over the musical spectrum – from Depeche Mode to Iron Maiden. Arcane Icelandic acts stand shoulder to shoulder with U2 online. Beatnik poets share bookshelf space with J. K. Rowling. The grand bazaar of the Internet becomes a Market of the Many, showing how extreme diversity is a more accurate and honest description of mankind than nationality or "normalcy" ever was.

## ● What product are you?

The Market of the Many. Five words that truly summarize the situation in most countries and industry segments today. Think about a supermarket. Rows and rows of goods. Categories with as many as twenty different brands. A plethora of choices in categories that used to be considered commodities, such as milk or flour. There's standard milk, low-fat milk, flavoured milk, organic milk, large and small packages, and that's just from one supplier. The supermarket can be used to symbolize anything from pension funds (high- or low-risk, ethical, geographic, and so on) to speaker agencies (want to hire the trendspotter, the motivational speaker, the musician or the ukulele-playing motivational trendspotter?). Everywhere we look, the range of choices is bordering on the infinite in some cases. Usually when someone starts an argument by pointing to the infinite number of choices, their ultimate goal is to make us feel bad, or at least admit how confusing infinite choice can

**People don't want to choose. They want exactly what they want**

be. That's not my belief. On the contrary, I believe that the Market of the Many makes people happier. The reason is that more choices enable people to choose exactly what they want. I call this *precision consumption.* If you're motivated by ethical investments or believe organic production is better for the environment, the ability to choose products and services that correspond to your personality will make you happier. Somebody else has different motivations and will make different choices. Choice is actually a myth. People don't want to choose. They want exactly what they want. They want precision consumption. Whatever. Whenever. Wherever. Let me illustrate with a personal experience from a time before precision consumption. I'm a big fan of the rock band Kiss, and when I was a young boy, this fandom bordered on fanaticism. I had to own everything they had ever made. In 1983, the band stopped using their signature make-up and released the album *Lick It Up*. This album was special because the sleeve was the first chance many of us had to see the band without make-up. There was no Google picture search with paparazzi images in those times. I had saved up some money and got on the bus to buy *Lick It Up*. It took me about thirty minutes to get to the record store. Once there, I waited in line for my turn and then put my 100-krona bill on the counter.

"I would like a copy of Kiss's *Lick It Up*," I said, and felt somewhat older than I was.

"I'm sorry, we're all sold out," said the clerk.

This is where I should have turned around and gone to another record store, but since we lived in the suburbs, the next nearest record store was a good half-hour away. Instead, I made one of my life's biggest mistakes so far and asked the clerk:

"Do you have anything else to recommend?"

Unfortunately he did.

"We have a really great new album by a band called the Thompson Twins." He smiled and held up *Into The Gap*.

I bought the album. Took the bus home. Put the record on and realized what a disastrous mistake I had made. It sounded nothing like Kiss. In fact, the Thompson Twins used keyboards, a definite no-no for heavy rock fans like me. I suffered through fifteen seconds of the album and then switched it off. Depressed. Only to be interrupted by my mum, who stuck her head into my room and said:

"That sounded nice!"

And she would keep doing that for the rest of the year: "Put on that nice album by those Twins," she'd say.

How I suffered.

What's it like when young boys and girls want to buy *Lick It Up* today?

All they do is surf online and press a button to buy any of Kiss's thirty albums. If they don't want the entire album, they cherry-pick certain songs. If they don't want to pay, they file-share.

I had to take the bus, in the snow (we had colder winters back then), and hear a "No!" when I wanted *Lick It Up*. Then suffer with the Thompson Twins for the greater part of a year.

It's a sign of ageing when you try to portray yourself as a victimized generation and claim that "the young of today have never had it so good".

Precision consumption not only saves time, effort and money. It also makes people happier or, at least, less discontented when they're forced to put up with second best (or the absolutely worst, as in my case). This is especially true when you look at migration across the world. People can precision-consume countries and cities. Where would you like to live right now? What suits the particular needs you may have at a particular life stage? If you can't see how that would make us happier, then consider the gay man born in a small rural village. Some decades ago, he would have been doomed to a life of bigotry and oppression. Now, he's free to leave and live in a place that reflects and tolerates his values, ideas and sexuality.

## ● Small company – big world

If you combine the trends discussed so far in the book – the gradual transformation of capitalism into favouring the individual over the collective and fragmentization – you get a typical portrait of the modern company. Fewer people are needed to do more things. Most companies have decreased the size of their workforce, but their market, especially the potential one, is bigger than ever. A good way to envision this is to imagine the company as a fried egg where yolk and white used to be of roughly equal size but where the yolk – the staff – has now shrunk and the white – the market and the outside world – has grown significantly. This has a particular implication for how business is conducted. I'll use a large company in the chemical industry to illustrate this change. This company has a long history of success. In the early 1990s, it employed more than 150,000 people around the world. Since then, the staff has been cut roughly in half. By outsourcing, downsizing and technological innovation. So far, so familiar. Their market has increased about tenfold, mainly through the addition of innovative new products and services. Here comes the twist. A decade ago, this company developed their own products, sold their own products and were convinced that few if anyone knew the chemical market as well as them. Nowadays, they don't develop a single product themselves, they sell all their products and services through agents and distributors and, because of this, they know that people outside the firm know a whole lot more about the chemical industry than they do themselves. This has changed the kinds of people that the company hires.

"Fifteen years ago," their HR director told me, "our dream employee was a young, aggressive, sales-oriented male. Someone who could represent our dominance in the market and not be afraid of boastfully pushing our products and services to customers around the world.

"Today," he added, "our dream employee is a quiet, slightly nerdy diplomat." Someone who can listen, build networks and foster strong relationships with all the partners that the company depends upon. The shift towards a smaller company operating in a bigger world has completely changed what type of personalities the company seeks and what type of work they're willing to reward. I share this anecdote because I believe a similar situation is facing virtually any company today. They're smaller and the world is bigger, and that changes everything in terms of how they should operate.

## ● Innovation reconsidered

Finding new ideas in companies, whether it was done in a long-term formalized process called "innovation" or over a coffee break and called "brainstorming", used to look something like this: a bunch of people sitting around, writing down as many ideas as they could on a blank sheet of paper. What then followed was either analysis (in the "brainstorming" sessions) or toll-gating (in the more extensive process of innovation). A hundred ideas were either analysed or toll-gated down to a handful of ideas. These ideas were often prototyped, and if they weren't shot down by top management – which was often the case – they tested their wings on the open market. In this world, many companies built R&D departments. Research and Development – hardly words that radiate the kind of speed and flexibility that the "small egg yolk/large egg white" companies described above

are looking for. Finding new ideas
**R and D should instead stand** while minimizing risk was the
**for "Rip-off" and "Duplicate"** very reason R&D departments
existed. In today's world – with

access to a myriad of products, services and solutions available at the touch of a button – companies should still have an R&D function but the two letters R and D should instead stand for "Rip off" and "Duplicate". Steal and copy ideas that already exist somewhere else in the world. In another market. In another industry. In another country. With a competitor. In the head of an entrepreneur. Instead of starting with a blank piece of paper, start with Google. Somebody out there has already solved the problem or opportunity you're facing, whether it's professional or personal. An inspiring example comes from the world of household chemicals. An executive of a consumer products company was worrying about how to make the bleach his company produces better. He thought it would be nice if the bleach didn't cause "collateral damage". That is, he wanted it to harm bad stuff without harming good stuff. He seized upon the notion of collateral damage and began to wonder where else collateral damage was a problem. Chemotherapy came to mind, and he visited some oncologists who gave him some ideas about what they did to make chemotherapy less harmful to patients. He then applied those same ideas to improve his company's bleach.[1]

This kind of R&D process is quicker and often enables people and companies to study a product or service that has already been launched in a live context. How's that for controlling risks?

Using the Market of the Many for your benefit is just one aspect of living, working and thriving in a fragmented world. Another aspect is the demands that this global marketplace makes.

## The hairdresser's syndrome

Most people have a hairdresser that they visit with some regularity. Mine is Mattias at Vattenkammade Snoken (the "Water-combed Snake") in the central part of Stockholm. Mattias is in his forties, friendly, not particularly hip (which tells you something about my pragmatic view of having my hair cut) and someone I have used faithfully for over a decade. As a service provider, Mattias can be summarized by the word "quite". He's quite good at what he does (even if my wife insists on teasing me for my constantly receding hairline). He's quite cheap, quite fast and quite nice to talk to (even if our conversations rarely stray far outside holiday plans and music). The interesting thing is that everything used to be just like Mattias. Your local bank was quite good. The local newspaper was quite fast in telling the latest stories. The bus drivers were, or at least should have been, quite nice. When the world was local, and by that I mean *only* local, everything could be characterized by the word "quite". In countries like Sweden – which thrived on national monopolies – many things were characterized by being bad, expensive, slow and rude. The closest I ever came to the miseries of the Third World was experiencing the children's programming on Sweden's two state-owned TV channels while growing up. They were limited to fifteen minutes per day and then usually consisted of ill-disguised left-wing propaganda in the form of flattering documentaries about the Soviet Union or Czechoslovakia. When people couldn't leave the country they were born in, physically or mentally, governments saw an opportunity to indoctrinate their population with the idea that they were living in Utopia and that the world outside was a dangerous place. The stories my wife tells me about growing up in Yugoslavia under Tito are even more remarkable than the things I encountered in Sweden. In Yugoslav schools, they would quiz young children about Tito's habits and about his dog, Rex. The best students in these quizzes would be awarded a trip to celebrate Tito's birthday in Belgrade, even though the dictator had been dead for some time.

Then something happened.

Although glasnost, economic liberalization, deregulation and connectivity have been described extensively in many other books, I'm still not certain about exactly what happened between the 1980s and the 1990s. Even when I add up all these facts and factor in things like the recession, there's still something missing. An X-factor of some sort. I believe, but cannot prove, that this X-factor was entrepreneurship. The combination of cheap credit, accessible technology and long-term suffering in markets closed off to the world outside introduced a new generation of people who wanted to change things. All over the world, a generation of change agents and entrepreneurs revolutionized television, telecoms, airlines, trains, banks, newspapers and most of the other things that had been characterized by being bad, slow, expensive and rude.

## ● Cheapest, fastest, nicest

Today, most people on earth live in a world that is interconnected, global and instantly accessible. Reading newspapers from other countries, buying mutual funds from foreign banks, choosing between hundreds of airlines – just look at the number of different tailfins at any airport – and sampling some of the hundreds of TV channels available over cable or satellite have become such ordinary, mundane activities that to draw attention to them would be to sound like an old man marvelling at the abundance of cheap food in a supermarket. The result of people having a choice is that "quite" doesn't get you as far as it used to. In most categories today, we search for the offering that is either the best, the cheapest, the fastest or the nicest. Hairdressers like Mattias are still fairly protected from this development since few people travel far to get their hair cut (outsourcing) and we haven't yet found a way to download a new haircut digitally. If we did, hairdressers like Mattias would face the same global competition that characterizes many other industries. He would either have to be the best damned hairdresser there is and fix such a stellar style for me that people stopped and turned in the street. Or he would have to be so cheap that he'd literally pay me money to have my hair cut. Or he would have to be so amazingly fast that I wouldn't even notice my hair had been cut. Or he would have to be so nice that every appointment started with a long embrace.

Whenever arguments like these are presented, some people voice concern that an elitist society is being created where those unable to be the best or the cheapest would be slowly but surely eliminated in a corporate survival of the fittest. Not true. As a matter of fact, you can thrive at the opposite end of the spectrum as well, by being the rudest or slowest or most expensive. Even the worst. Here are some examples.

More and more companies want to hire rude people that they call "rebels" who'll spend their days heckling people and challenging the status quo inside the corporation. An American company I spoke to were willing to pay up to 100,000 dollars per year each for these people. There are even consultancies that have corporate rebels for hire ready to rudely and bluntly pinpoint all the shortcomings in an organization for the purpose of making it better.

We've also seen in the past decade how slowness is becoming a market in and of itself. In a fast, hectic world, people seek refuge in slow activities. Slow food – the art of cooking and eating slowly – is one example. The most common potato breeds in Sweden are called "Turbo", "Speed" and "Rocket". They're bred and adapted to a marketplace that wants potatoes to mature quickly. The result looks and feels just like a potato but tastes pretty bland compared to its slowly grown cousins. A slow workout is the antidote to quick, sweaty gym sessions with one rep designed to take fifteen minutes or more. Or how about some slow sex?

We also see that the most expensive offerings also thrive in a world where people are willing to pay more for things if they're organic, or have an interesting story, or are well crafted and designed. We'll pay more to sit at the front of the plane. Or if the speed of the broadband connection will knock our socks off. And so on.

My favourite example, however, is that people who are extremely bad at something are able to make a career out of this in today's world. Think of all the YouTube stars and *X-Factor* contestants who become famous not because they display superior skills but, on the contrary, because they show off their ineptitude. Some of these people even earn money through sponsorship or launch a career after millions of people have laughed at (or is it with?) their misfortune. The conclusion is that you can thrive by either being the best or the worst at something. The fastest or the slowest. The nicest or the rudest. The cheapest or the most expensive.

The Swedish notion "*Lagom*" – meaning being in the middle of something, neither hot nor cold – is what you want to stay away from.

## ● Being boundaryless

Just because the world's boundaries are coming down doesn't mean people adapt easily to the new situation. Boundaries are a convenient way of distancing yourself from others and setting yourself apart. I'm Swedish and you're not. Engineers enjoy working with other engineers. Companies claim that they and their industry are "special". And so on. This kind of entrenched behaviour, convenient as it is, may even be detrimental in the increasingly open mindset and landscape of the modern world. Al-Qaeda and the banking crisis of 2008 are just two recent examples of what happens when you have too many like-minded men working together.

When I went to business school, I noticed that the walls of the toilets were full of graffiti, sometimes artfully done. One way of interpreting this is that people at the business school wanted to create even though they were stuck studying accountancy and organizational strategy during the day. On the surface, they were business school students, but underneath some of them were artists, writers and provocateurs. Something happens mentally, though, when you're grouped together with other people and given a label. The famous example is, of course, when a bunch of people chosen at random were given the role of either prisoner or prison warden and the experiment had to be called off after just a few days because the "prison wardens" became too brutal in their treatment of the prisoners. I've had a similar if less dramatic experience of this type of mind corruption. I teach a course at the Stockholm School of Entrepreneurship which is open to students of four different schools: a business school, an art school, an engineering institute and a medical school. The students are young and have about two years of study behind them when they enrol on my course, so you would assume that they were still open minded. That is alarmingly often not the case. On the contrary, you will often hear the business school students make remarks like "What do we need the other students for? They don't know how to use PowerPoint." The engineers keep complaining because they feel my course in trendspotting and future thinking is too shallow. "We want to go deeper, into the process of things," they'll say. The art students are continually frustrated and ask when they'll get to actually *do* something, not just talk. Finally, the med students tend to drop out because they feel the course isn't important enough. It isn't life or death, after all.

> **Boundaries are a convenient way of distancing yourself from others and setting yourself apart**

What these students – as well as bankers and al-Qaeda terrorists – need to learn and embrace if they want to thrive in the coming decades is working and thinking across disciplines – from the creative fields to the number-crunching fields (in the case of al-Qaeda, it's more a question of putting yourself in the shoes of the potential victim, but that may be asking too much of them). The case for interdisciplinary work isn't just built on touchy-feely arguments about solidarity and compassion; it's also an economic one. Allocating people to a certain title and role may be efficient, and when efficiency is a key focus for a company, that's a logical step to take. Nowadays, however, the focus is increasingly on *effectiveness* – not just doing things right but finding and doing the right things. Effectiveness tends to thrive in companies that also embrace creativity, risk-taking and a great deal of personal freedom for their employees. When the landscape is predictable and the competition fairly straightforward, focus on efficiency. In the opposite case, which we see in many industries currently, a greater emphasis should be put on effectiveness. Companies operating on this kind of terrain need to organize themselves differently, and a good place to start is the project model. Project, as you may be aware, comes from Latin's *pro jicere* – to throw things forward – and the form is perfect for the types of risky experiments needed when times are turbulent. The popular metaphor often used by people favouring the project model is Hollywood, where film teams assemble for one production and then disperse, regroup and work on the next thing. What's lacking from this metaphor, though, is the "how" – *how* do these teams actually work? How are they able to quickly become productive in the company of relative strangers? The answer lies in something called "swift trust"[2] – fostering and maintaining a culture where trust can quickly be established and you don't have to spend a lot of time on team-building exercises.

> Nowadays, however, the focus is increasingly on *effectiveness*

Corporate walls aren't the only ones coming down. With the rise of online collaboration between strangers, we are witnessing the rise of "invisible firms" that have no governance, no formal boundaries, not even a name. When these kinds of competitors arise, it may be useful to remind yourself that the word competition comes from the Latin *com petare* – to strive together. Tear down the walls, open up your company and say ahhh …

## Seeing through the matrix

In the 1999 science fiction film *The Matrix*, the world is an illusion created by machines and only a small number of individuals have the gift to see through this "matrix". This is a perfect symbol for what we see happening in the world right now. Nations, borders and industry boundaries were created by someone at some point to serve a specific purpose. They are tools – not laws of nature – and when they fail to be useful, they crumble and disappear, which is what we currently see happening in the world. Or rather, what we *should* see happening in the world but, just as in *The Matrix*, the number of people who can see through the illusion of a nation or the porous boundaries of a particular industry is quite small. Most of us are happy to go with the flow and see the world through a lens full of borders. Some even go so far as to see any threat to the idea of nations as a threat to themselves, and are therefore prone to fight it. Nationalist politics is one sign of this. Nationalist parties will usually talk some gibberish about "keeping a race clean from contamination". Unfortunately for them, the future will be all about "contamination" – of blood and in business. Just as we can't see the atoms moving inside a rock, we cannot see the millions of minuscule changes that take place in life and society on a daily basis. Grown-ups tend to think that the world is just as it was when they were growing up, and that everything happening now is an exception. As if the world will somehow revert back to what it looked like several years ago, and that this was somehow a better society to live in. Tell that to all the people who were oppressed by "normalcy" – the homosexual born in the small village, for instance. Or to industries that were closed off to women. Or to people who didn't have their own nation-state – like Assyrians, Kurds or Armenians. The world we're entering – as yet invisible to some people – will be bigger, better and certainly different from the version we've been living in.

# The Trendspotter Mission Manual

Want to be just like Keanu Reeves's Neo in *The Matrix*? Here's how:

STOP USING THE WORD "NORMAL" IMMEDIATELY!
IT'S A REMNANT FROM A SMALL WORLD FULL OF
BORDERS. THESE DAYS, THE WORLD IS A GLOBAL PLACE
FULL OF UNIQUE, QUIRKY PEOPLE AND PLACES.

INVENT NEW METAPHORS!
THE HUMAN BRAIN NEEDS SIMPLE, TANGIBLE METAPHORS
TO UNDERSTAND ABSTRACT THINGS, AND TO NAME
SOMETHING IS TO CLAIM IT. THE METAPHOR DOESN'T
EVEN HAVE TO BE CORRECT. NEW YORK TIMES
COLUMNIST THOMAS FRIEDMAN HAS WRITTEN A
BESTSELLING BOOK CALLED THE WORLD IS FLAT,
AND THAT TITLE IS A REMARKABLY INACCURATE CLAIM.

GET OUT OF YOUR COMFORT ZONE!
MAKE SURE YOU VISIT AT LEAST
ONE NEW COUNTRY EVERY YEAR
AND MEET PEOPLE FROM
EMERGING INDUSTRIES ONCE A
MONTH. THE ULTIMATE BLINDER IS
YOUR DAILY ROUTINE, AND IF THAT
NEVER CHANGES, YOU'LL MISS
MOST OF WHAT'S HAPPENING IN
THE WORLD OUT THERE.

PRECISION-CONSUME!
BUY MEDIA AND READ BLOGS FROM THE FRINGES OF
SOCIETY. SAMPLE UNKNOWN BRANDS. TRAVEL TO
PLACES NOBODY HAS HEARD OF. SMALL IS BEAUTIFUL!

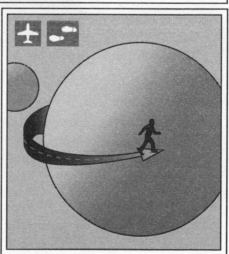

GO GLOBAL!
NO MATTER WHO YOU ARE OR WHAT YOU DO, START
SELLING YOURSELF INTERNATIONALLY. IT'S EASIER AND
CHEAPER THAN EVER.

# 3 A shock to the senses

## How information abundance has left us clueless

*Information is not knowledge, knowledge is not wisdom, and wisdom is not foresight.*

– Arthur C. Clarke

# The 30-metre book pile

Imagine yourself driving on a Continental motorway somewhere in Europe. You're heading towards Belgium. Several miles from the border, you notice something strange on the horizon. The previously flat country seems to have grown a mountain since you were last there. Not in fact a mountain but an entire wall. At least 30 metres high. As you get closer, you notice that the wall isn't made of rock but of something else completely. It seems to be some kind of mosaic pattern. Wait! Could it really be? Yes, it is. The wall – stretching across the entire horizon – is entirely made of books. Millions and millions of paperback books. The wall is thick. Extremely thick. In fact, it makes up the entire area of Belgium. Where there was previously a country of exquisite food and political tension, there is now just one giant pile of paperback novels.

This is merely a fantasy, but it illustrates the explosive growth of information that we have experienced in the past decade. One paperback novel, from Ian McEwan's *Saturday* to Khaled Hosscini's *The Kite Runner*, equals one megabyte of information. At the time of writing this in 2008, the amount of information in the world is roughly equal to 281

**The amount of information in the world is roughly equal to 281 billion gigabytes**

billion gigabytes.[1] That is an unfathomable number, but if you use the book metaphor, it is equal to a book pile 6 metres high covering all of Belgium. It grows exponentially, however, so in just a few years, this pile will exceed 20 metres. More information will be produced in these few years than has been accumulated in the world up to and including 2008. And it just keeps going. Writing and publishing a book in this information inferno seems as silly as exporting sand to the Sahara. The world could hardly need yet another book. Or a magazine. Or an article. Or an e-mail. Right? The reality is not that simple.

This chapter will focus on what happens to people when change is rapid and unexpected. The explosive growth of information along with the rise of the World Wide Web serves as a suitable example. Furthermore, the chapter will focus on how people tend to misinterpret sudden changes and thereby miss far more important, underlying shifts.

## ● The moonwalking bear

A recent television commercial showed two street basketball teams with about four people each. A deadpan voiceover declared this to be an "awareness test" and asked us to count the number of passes that the team dressed in white jerseys made. Someone yelled "Go!" and both teams were off, passing a basketball to each other in some sort of strange variety of basketball that seemed to involve only passing and a lot of running around. Counting the passes was tricky, but as I sat glued to the television, I was able to count the correct number, not without a sense of pride. "The correct number is thirteen," said the voiceover. "But … did you see the moonwalking bear?" What? The film sequence was quickly rewound and the passing game started over again. There it was. Walking or rather dancing in plain view among the players was someone dressed in a bear costume doing a mediocre rendition of Michael Jackson's famous moonwalking dance. I had missed it. Judging by many other people's reactions, so had they.

This clip – or its more famous predecessor produced by the Visual Cognition Lab at the University of Illinois – is an excellent example of what happens when we're busy focusing on certain things – the team in white passing the ball – and miss other things – the moonwalking bear. How does this relate to the information boom in the past decade? The human mind is an apparatus designed to focus on things. Simply try any kind of meditation where the goal is to purge your mind of any particular thought and you will experience just how focus driven the brain is. We want to think about certain things. We want to busy our mind with something specific, something particular. Why else would people read books? And why would they want these books to be structured and somewhat coherent and not just a messy stream of consciousness?

If we think about this in the long term, the parallel between the invisible moonwalking bear and the information boom becomes even more apparent. People learn to see the world a certain way, and very few of us are good at *unlearning* what we know. Our mind works as if it were on a trajectory where the lessons we learn at a younger age are assumed to be true as we grow older. People

**People learn to see the world a certain way, and very few of us are good at *unlearning* what we know**

who grew up before the emergence of the Web tend to see information as something solid (a magazine, a piece of paper, a book, and so on), and in many instances as something rare and valuable. Take the example of pornography. Growing up without Internet access – and being male – I have experienced how finding pornography is a highly demanding endeavour (who on earth would ever walk into a newsagent and buy a pornographic magazine?). We had to search in the forest or climb into skips to find a few torn magazine pages of XXX-rated fare that we could gaze over. The exercise had less to do with sexual arousal than with the treasure hunt aspect. Today, pornography is available for free, twenty-four hours per day, at the touch of a button. Given the existence of spam, you may not even have to touch any buttons as the pornography finds you instead via e-mail. Information has been transformed from being rare, valuable and finite into something abundant, free and all encompassing (where does a news story end online?). As this new kind of information is abstract, however, many people cling to the old idea of what information is – often without knowing they are doing so – and just multiply it. That's what I did with the metaphor of Belgium being covered by paperback books. In reality, the information boom is not about an exponential growth in the number of paperbacks published but about information being radically transformed from finite products into an endless, ongoing process. We fail to see this moonwalking bear (a new kind of information) because we count the number of passes instead (the old way of looking at information). Statisticians talk about *differences in degree* – where there's just more or less of something – and *differences in kind* – where something has changed fundamentally. The information boom that we've witnessed over the past decade is an example of where a radical difference in degree (the information boom) has created a difference in kind (information has become an endless, ongoing process).[2]

If you update the hardware on your computer, it will be faster, safer, more stable, even more fun and less irritating to use. If you update and change the software, it will seem incomprehensible for a while. As many of us know, even the hardware is prone to crash if we radically adjust the software we're using. Mental software adjustment – unlearning – is painful and tends to be something most people avoid. Learning to live with change is just too demanding and too energy consuming. Our mental software tends to lag behind "hardware development" – changes in the real world.

A very interesting example of this is the shift from socialist economic models to capitalist economic models in eastern Europe since the fall of the Berlin Wall in 1989. On a hardware level, what happened is fairly straightforward. All of a sudden, everything cost money and the price basically reflected the demand and attractiveness of the product offered. Anyone vacationing in Croatia in the past few years will have experienced this. The prices for car rental, hotel rooms and restaurants rival those of cities that have been capitalist a lot longer. The case of Croatia is interesting, though, because it also illustrates lagging mental software. In the late 1990s, Croatia's tourist board decided to create a marketing strategy for the young republic. They decided that the target group for all Croatia's tourist efforts should be the "Cultural Traveller" – an affluent, older traveller interested in the comfort, authenticity and quality of life that Croatia believed it could offer. New five-star hotels were built, as well as restaurants and other infrastructure changes to cater to this coveted group of travellers. The people who tended to flock to Croatia in droves, however, were Czech and Polish backpackers, as well as convoys of Italian cars carrying families who wanted to see the other side of the Adriatic Sea. These groups were very far from the targeted Cultural Traveller, and they tended to bring their own food and live in campsites. Croatia boomed as a tourist destination but for all the wrong reasons in the eyes of the tourist board. That's when they made the disastrous decision – with the help of the government – to prohibit people from bringing their own food into Croatia. The rationale was simple. No food, no backpackers, and that would again let Croatia focus on attracting the "right" people. In reality, neighbouring tourist magnets like Italy and Greece were all too happy to receive the clientele who preferred bringing their own food on holiday. Croatia abandoned Plan A but their Plan B is even more telling about the difficulty of adapting to capitalism. To offset the effects of attracting the "wrong" clientele, many of the hotels and restaurants charged a higher price to be able to meet their high budget targets. Demand fell and, strangely, prices increased. As any recent visitor to Croatia can attest, it is a country with a stunning landscape and plenty of empty but expensive restaurants and hotels.[3]

What this example serves to illustrate is that adapting a market economy and learning to use it are two different things. The hardware (the market system) preceded the software (learning to use it). The same thing is true for information. We have been living in an information-abundant society for more than a decade, yet much of our behaviour is still similar to what it was before the rise of the World Wide Web: from schools basing teaching on memorization to people reading physical newspapers. Software lags behind hardware. Digital information transfer follows Moore's Law,[4] while collective human behaviour tags along at a much slower pace.

Another example of this laggard effect is the changes to food supply in many parts of the world in the twentieth century. With the rise of industrial agriculture and global markets, food has gone from being a scarcity to being available 24/7. More specifically, things that were once considered rare and valuable, such as fatty food and sugar, have become something we can sample – even indulge in – on every street corner any day of the year. This supply has failed to be translated into a change in our eating behaviour, however. We still celebrate Thanksgiving, Christmas and other holidays with tables full of fat and sugar. Culturally conditioned behaviour and habits are lagging behind supply-side changes.

With the information supply continuing to grow at a furious pace, what are some of the lessons we need to learn in order to better adapt and avoid some of the pitfalls that abundant information creates?

## ● Addicted to lies, sensations and really bad news

Sex feels good. This is a statement few people would disagree with. As a matter of fact, according to recent studies in happiness, sexual intercourse is one of the most effective means of finding and sustaining higher levels of well-being. This is something we should be grateful for. Imagine if sex made us suffer severe physical pain or caused depression by merely thinking about it. In that case, it would be safe to assume that very few people would engage in sexual encounters and the number of offspring produced would be significantly lower. In fact, some would even argue that the survival of mankind hinges upon the biological mechanisms that make sex so pleasant and enjoyable.

A similar relationship exists within information. Can you recite pi to six hundred decimals? Or even six? Probably not. The reasons are numerous. It may be cumbersome to memorize more than a few digits; the actual utility of doing so may seem unclear to most people; and – above all – the very idea of discussing pi or memorizing more than the basic components of it is so exquisitely boring that we prefer learning to yoyo or drinking a can of Diet Coke instead. This is important. Learning to yoyo has great social utility – people gawking when you show off your tricks – and drinking a caffeinated beverage gives us instant gratification. Engaging the mind in the

**We prefer sexy lies to boring truths**

seemingly meaningless activity of memorizing random digits has neither of these characteristics (to most people) so we tend not to do it. The kind of information we do like to engage in includes things that are similar to yoyoing or drinking Diet Coke. We love gossip. We love sensational rumours. We love really bad news (for other people). We prefer sexy lies to boring truths. This becomes problematic when we have all kinds of information available at our fingertips. Studying the most frequently searched words and terms on a variety of search engines shows that most people prefer rumours and slander concerning celebrity endeavours to the arcane secrets of pi.

An interesting academic study showed just why this works so predictably. People were exposed to two different groups of pictures. One group featured mysterious landscapes and interesting faces. The other one featured boring pictures of clocks and car parks. That people preferred the first group is hardly surprising. The interesting part was that brain scans showed increased production of the brain's pleasure-enhancing neurotransmitters (called opioids) when the subjects watched mysterious landscapes and interesting faces.[5] When people were left to sift through pictures for themselves, many could sit for a long time and just gaze at the dopamine-inducing pictures. We are, in essence, addicted to certain kinds of information.

This might explain why "few people have the wisdom to prefer the criticism that would do them good, to the praise that deceives them", as the French author François de la Rochefoucauld once remarked.

## ● Why are there so many cars in the Maldives?

The Maldives is many people's idea of paradise. Sandy beaches and crystal-clear waters spread across hundreds of coral atolls, most of which are so small that they can be explored on foot within an hour. The capital, Malé, occupies an island that spans 2 by 2 kilometres. Minuscule by most measurements. Interestingly, in the past decade this Lilliputian capital has been invaded by cars. Lots and lots of cars. The traffic has become so bad on certain days that not only has walking become a faster alternative; walking back and forth to your destination several times is possible in the time many spend stuck in traffic. The question every visitor is bound to ask himself is why this situation arose. As recently as the mid-1990s, very few cars could be found in Malé.[6] Going from no cars to fully fledged traffic jams has occurred in numerous emerging economies around the world. To find out why, all you have to do is look at yourself and then look around you. What are you wearing? What are other people wearing? Chances are that there are many overlaps in what you've decided to wear today and what many in your vicinity are also wearing, be it T-shirts or bow ties. If you're naked in bed by yourself, that's even more telling. Why are you naked? The answer is that you got this idea from someone and then copied it. You didn't invent the idea that sleep should be met with very few clothes on. Neither did you invent the T-shirt or the bow tie. You copied these ideas too. From whom is irrelevant and, in many cases, impossible to say. Similarly, Malé didn't invent the automobile or the concept that a city should contain them. Malé merely copied this idea from most

Imitation is the sincerest form of trend-spreading

other cities around the world, just as people copy ideas from other people. To put it another way, information is contagious. Imitation is the sincerest form of trend-spreading. Trendy ideas may be the ultimate manifestation of this, but the reality is that virtually anything we see, use and think was invented by someone else. From quantum physics to black mascara. The danger of this viral form of information-spreading is that the wrong (as in "untruthful") ideas can spread as easily as the right (as in "factually correct") ideas can, and sometimes even more easily.

This is apparent in the online world, where sensational news can spread around the world in an instant, even though it doesn't have a trace of truth in it. The effects are worrying. An experiment showed that when people were exposed to a certain piece of information repeatedly, they were more prone to accept it as fact.[7] In other words, if people are subjected to some vicious insult, unscientific speculation or juicy piece of gossip time and time again, they are more likely to think that the insult, the speculation or the gossip is actually truthful. Regurgitating information without checking its validity has even been given a name: *churnalism*, a hybrid of churn and journalism.[8]

## ● Succeeding in the knowledge economy

An interesting article a few years ago, called "The asshole in the corner office", made the point that people would rather work with someone friendly and mediocre than with a brilliant asshole. This should come as no surprise given the aforementioned arguments. It also points to a worrying fact. In today's information-abundant world, dubbed the "Knowledge Economy", being nice, outgoing and pleasant to be around is often mistaken as being competent and skilled. We tend to trust who is saying something rather than scrutinizing what they are actually saying. I call this the "Hoa Hoa" phenomenon. Hoa Hoa used to be a Swedish weightlifter and is now quite famous for being a regular on game shows in Sweden. He tends to win because he knows a lot of trivia, the skill that gets rewarded by game shows and in dinner-table conversations. Many admire these kinds of qualities. To be a raconteur and good at conversation and listening are traits that have high social utility. These traits, however, don't necessarily translate into any kind of economic utility. Being nice is not equal to being productive or innovative. Think about Yoda instead. The small, green savant in the Star Wars movies is probably not invited to many dinner parties. In fact, he seems incapable of small talk and his wisdom tends to cause frustration before it enlightens. The societal and commercial utility of a Yoda is infinitely greater than that of a Hoa Hoa, but when it comes to social utility the situation is reversed. This can cause problems. A well-known fact for many doctors is that they sometimes avoid subjecting patients they like to uncomfortable treatments. In the worst cases, this worsens disease and can make certain symptoms go unnoticed. When we live in a world that prefers Hoa Hoas instead of Yodas, we become less productive and, more importantly, fail to discover certain things.

> **Being nice is not equal to being productive or innovative**

## ● An information diet

If I were to write down a number of things that are important to me in the world, there would be several strange bullet points on that list: my wife, my sons, my family and so on. I describe them as "strange" because when I start thinking about the list that other people would make, I assume that few others would put "Magnus's wife, his sons and his family" on that list. They are more likely to list people and things they care about themselves. The world that I see and the things that I value are not identical to the world that other people see and the things they value. A disproportionate number of people, things and phenomena of personal importance skew my perspective. We can call this the "Spousal Obstruction Syndrome" (SOS), and it's one of the reasons why people just cannot come to an agreement on certain issues. It's a well-known fact that people can watch the exact same football game and see two completely different stories being played out, depending on which side they cheer for. Similarly, many conflicts in the world remain unresolved because of SOS. "They started it so why should we try to resolve it?" The solution to this can be called the Spouse Denial Perspective. We need to continuously make an effort to fill our brain not just with things that feel good, are simple and trigger our opioids, but information that is inconvenient, complex, boring and uncomfortable to digest – an information diet of sorts. This is a parallel to the 1960s, when fat and sugar had become abundant and the diet pyramid was constructed, urging people to consume fibre, fruit and vegetables as well as fat and sugar.

Implementing an information diet is a strong justification for having compulsory schooling. What schools should put less empha-sis on, however, is memory. The

**What schools should put less emphasis on is memory**

reason is that memory is being continually devalued by the surge of Moore's Law. A person reads about 10 megabytes of text every day, hears 400 megabytes of sound and watches around 1 megabyte per second flashing before their eyes. That amount of information is basically available for free today, and within the next few years everything a person reads, hears and sees within an entire lifetime will be available in a device smaller than a mobile phone.[9] If schools still stress the value of memorizing things, they will be outpaced by technology. Teaching people to handle information the right way and to follow an information diet regimen should be the new calling of the school system – teaching people that scepticism is a virtue or, even better, to use the Roman adage "*cui bono*?" as a guide. Who benefits from this information?

Who benefits from me passing it on? What may the ulterior motives be? To put it in the words of a sixteenth-century cardinal: "Be very careful what you get into that head, because you will never get it out."

## ● Jolted

Whenever change is rapid and sudden, it is natural for us to be slow in changing our ways. We are, after all, routine-seeking creatures who value convenience. When things are very sudden and unexpected – say, a moonwalking bear dancing among two teams bouncing basketballs – they become invisible, and when they're invisible, we don't even know we should be adapting.

Most people tend to complain that there's too much information available today and don't think about how this abundance should be mastered and how we need to alter our information consumption accordingly. That is the other, invisible side of the information revolution. I found a way of dealing with it just as I had become a father for the first time. Before parenthood, my life and my career were intimately intertwined in a messy hybrid. I travelled, I spoke to people, I read books and blogs, and these things were done both for amusement and to discover new trends. Parenthood turned my life into a 24/7 workplace where blogs and plane trips were exchanged for sleepless nights and nappy changes. I had lost my old working habits and I imagined my career as a trendspotter would go down the drain.

Then one day – as I was walking the twins so my wife could get some sleep – I made a remarkable discovery. We had been given the disastrous advice by a friend to buy a single pram for the kids to share, the result being lots of tears every time we tried to put both kids to sleep in it. One child wanted to be awake and kick the other one, who wanted to sleep, and vice versa. On this particular walk, I had had enough. One child was asleep in the pram while I carried the other one in a harness. I held his little hand as he slept. That was when it hit me. How many times per year do we shake somebody's hand? The answer is bound to be quite a few. It's a boring, everyday exercise, and many people would be hard pressed to recall the name and face of the person they shook hands with after some time has passed. But as I was holding my son's hand, I realized what a profound difference that made.

## Holding hands with information generates new ways of thinking

Holding somebody's hand is something we rarely do, but when it happens, we feel something. We may feel something warm, funny, interesting or strange. We may feel attraction or repulsion. It doesn't really matter *what* we feel, the point is that we *do* feel. A boring everyday exercise – shaking hands – is transformed into a catalyst for all these kinds of feelings within a matter of seconds.

Information consumption functions the same way. Most of the time, we are so busy turning the page, deleting the e-mail or switching channels that we don't stop and reflect "What does this mean?" For me? For my life? For my business? Shaking hands with information is what we do on a daily basis. My insight was that holding hands with information – pausing for reflection, if only for a little while – generates new ways of thinking and enables you to utilize information in completely new ways. That is my way of approaching the mountain of information that is bombarding us on a daily basis. To quote Jonathan Haidt from his book *The Happiness Hypothesis*: "Quantity undermines the quality of our engagement. With such a vast and wonderful spread out before us, we often skim books or just read the reviews. We might have already encountered the Greatest Idea, the insight that would have transformed us had we savoured it, taken it to heart, and worked it into our lives."[10]

# The Trendspotter Mission Manual

Learning to live with change is a lot more demanding than merely understanding the change itself. Here's how you can make the information boom work to your advantage.

**CREATE AN INFORMATION DIET.**
DEFINE A LIST OF SOURCES THAT ARE NEW AND CONTINUALLY CHANGE IT. MAKE AN EFFORT TO CONSUME INFORMATION THAT IS SLOW, CUMBERSOME, COMPLEX AND SEEMINGLY UNINTERESTING.

**SEVEN SECONDS OF REFLECTION.**
MAKE IT A POINT TO STOP AND REFLECT ON A DAILY BASIS. WHAT CAN YOU DO WITH WHAT YOU'VE SEEN, HEARD OR READ TODAY? HOW CAN IT HELP YOU SOLVE THE ISSUES, PROBLEMS AND CHALLENGES YOU OR SOMEBODY ELSE IS CURRENTLY FACING?

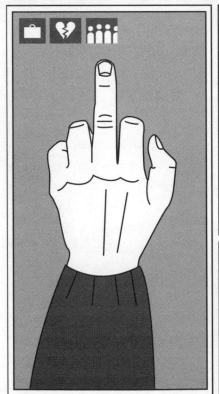

**WORK WITH PEOPLE YOU DON'T LIKE.**
IT MAY SEEM MASOCHISTIC, BUT FORCING YOURSELF INTO THE COMPANY OF PEOPLE WHO DON'T APPEAL TO YOU DIRECTLY MAY HELP YOU TO SEE NEW PERSPECTIVES AND, MORE IMPORTANTLY, WORK WITH SOME REALLY BRILLIANT PEOPLE.

**TRACE COPIED IDEAS!**
VIRTUALLY ANY IDEA OR OPINION WE ENCOUNTER WAS COPIED FROM SOMEWHERE ELSE. MAKE IT A POINT TO FIND OUT FROM WHERE THESE MEMES — IDEA VIRUSES — ORIGINATE. THIS IS EASY ON BLOGS, WHERE SOURCES ARE USUALLY HYPERLINKED, BUT MAY BE A LITTLE MORE DIFFICULT IN OTHER CONTEXTS. THIS WILL ENABLE YOU TO GET A BIGGER PICTURE OF WHAT SOURCES TEND TO INFLUENCE MANY PEOPLE.

**BE INCOMPETENT!**
MARKETING AUTHOR SETH GODIN ONCE CLAIMED THAT COMPETENT PEOPLE RESIST CHANGE, SINCE ALL THEY WANT TO DO IS LOOK GOOD AND SEEM COMPETENT, WHICH THEY CANNOT DO WHEN TOO MANY THINGS ARE CHANGING AROUND THEM. MAKE IT A POINT TO BE INCOMPETENT AND PROUDLY PROCLAIM: "I DON'T KNOW!" WHENEVER SOCIETY CHANGES, THE WAY IT HAS DONE IN THE PAST DECADE.

# 4 The trend illusion

## How a faster world forces us to use our imagination

*When you can't imagine how things are going to change, that doesn't mean nothing will change. It means that things will change in ways that are unimaginable*

– Bruce Sterling

## Screeching to a halt

The economic slowdown and banking collapse in 2008 were, despite media headlines, not unique. Financial crises have occurred with some regularity throughout history. What was surprising, though, was the speed with which this slowdown occurred. "Screeching to a halt" was one particularly popular formulation used by commentators and editorial columnists. "Slamming on the brakes" was another. This is how *McKinsey Quarterly* described it:

The future of capitalism is here, and it's not what any of us expected. With breathtaking speed, in the autumn of 2008, the credit markets ceased functioning normally, governments around the world began nationalizing financial systems and considering bailouts of other troubled industries, and major independent US investment banks disappeared or became bank holding companies. Meanwhile, currency values, as well as oil and other commodity prices, lurched wildly, while housing prices in Spain, the United Kingdom, the United States, and elsewhere continued to slide.[1]

The speedy transition from boom to bust was seemingly unrivalled and reinforced the popular notion that many things tend to happen a lot faster nowadays. This idea is not new. The *Atlantic Journal* famously published the following passage to comment on the present situation:

The world is too large for us. Far too much is going on, too many crimes, too much violence, and too much stir. No matter how hard you try, you will lose the race. It is a constant struggle to try to keep up ... and instead you lose your foothold.

Science is pouring its findings over us so quickly that you jump between them in hopeless attempts to try to understand. The political world relies on a steady stream of fast news, so fast that you lose your breath trying to keep up with who's in and who's not. In the end the result is too much pressure on each and every one of us. The human being cannot cope with much more than this.[2]

Most people will recognize at least parts of this argument as being a somewhat accurate portrayal of life in the early 2000s. The quote, interestingly, was in fact written in 1852.

This chapter will look at what happens when changes are not just fast and surprising but incomprehensible and abstract too. What happens when we have a problem formulating what it is we see taking place before our eyes, which was the case in the early days of the financial meltdown.

## ● The vanishing point

Take a moment to complete the following sequence of numbers:

$$2, 4, \ldots, \ldots$$

There are a number of correct answers to this question, but your answer shows how your mind thinks about change.

The first – and to many most obvious – answer is "2, 4, 6, 8". This is an example of linear change, increasing by two units each time.

**Trends are usually thought of as being linear**

Trends are usually thought of as being linear, and when asked to explain how they visualize a trend, most people would describe some sort of curve or arrow pointing in a certain direction.

The second correct answer is "2, 4, 8, 16", wherein the units double. This is accelerated change, which is as far as most people go in terms of thinking about trends. A common metaphor is that of a forest fire that picks up pace as it grows larger and stronger.

The third answer, and the one that is invisible to many, is "2, 4, 16, 256". This is exponential change, where each unit is squared – multiplied by itself. Most people can visualize the J-shaped exponential curve but very few people are able to think in exponential terms.

**What happens when change is so fast that we can literally blink and miss it?**

What happens when change is so fast that we can literally blink and miss it? This is where a "trend illusion" comes in. The first two numerical examples, wherein change is linear or near-linear and quite predictable, tend to be thought of in terms of "trends". When it comes to exponential change, people are blind. Nobody talked about the "terrorism trend" before 11 September 2001. Nobody talked about the "banking crisis" trends before September 2008. We are inclined to see the events that signify these dates as being sudden and chaotic, which is the kind of trick that exponential change can play on our minds. Al-Qaeda had struck several times before 9/11, but it was on that September morning that awareness of them skyrocketed. The intricate web of factors that contributed to the financial chaos in 2008 had been burning slowly at the fringes of society for some time, yet took us by surprise when they all came together and exploded within a few weeks. "Trend" is what we name something we want to control, measure and exploit. This kind of trendspotting is useless when it comes to exponential change, so we need new and different tools in such a climate. I will get into those later in the chapter, but I will begin by focusing on the society that speed builds and the speedy society we now live in.

# ● The millisecond market

At business school, I was taught about the concept of insider trading, whereby somebody unlawfully exploits information about a certain stock for their own benefit. The underlying assumption was that you had plenty of time in which to conduct this kind of trading. Today, stock markets move in milliseconds. The reason is that a significant proportion of the trades are made not by humans but by lines of computer code known as algorithms. To simplify things, think of an algorithm as a small computer program that functions like a primitive human mind. It follows an "if x then y" way of reasoning. "If the stock reaches five hundred dollars then sell." In contrast to the primitive mind, the algorithm is able to do this at great speed. Someone once said about humans that "we live our lives in three-second intervals",[3] a comment on the amount of time it takes for the brain to get from thinking about a certain task ("I want to grab that pen", for example) to actually doing it. Algorithms live in a world of milliseconds. While your brain is organizing commands to get you to actually grab that pen, they have made hundreds of stock trades based on minuscule price shifts. The result is that we have stock markets that outpace the human mind and where profits and losses are made not in minutes but in a fraction of a second. A potential insider trader wouldn't even be able to gasp at the stock tip he received – much less act upon it – before it was too late. This is one of the reasons why the banking crisis in 2008 came so damn fast. We were dealing with markets operated in part by machines that had no respect for the emotional side of a downturn.

**We live our lives in three-second intervals**

Millisecond markets shift the balance of power to those who are quick. This has caused many stock brokerages to physically move closer to market servers in order to be able to capitalize on the milliseconds that the closer broadband connection enables.[4]

We see something similar happening in the world of digital gaming. Online role-playing games thrive on speed. A quick broadband connection is the difference between killing or being killed in certain games, which is why broadband-intensive countries like South Korea or Sweden tend to excel when world championships of online games are played.

This acceleration of society is frowned upon by many. Economists argue that the general level of welfare would rise if stock markets just slowed down a little bit, and the elderly, as always, complain that the young do everything too fast. The Luddite would obviously blame the rise of new technology and see the humans as victims. It's important to note, however, that humans drive this development themselves. We have an inherent need for speed. An enlightening example is the world of online news. A few years ago, a water main failed in New York City, exploded and left a giant crater in midtown. Google News, a news aggregator that links to the news stories of other providers, noticed that the first stories about the event came within minutes of the actual explosion. Local newspapers and TV stations in New York had their teams on the scene that quickly. But those minutes are an eternity for the people who started Googling the words "explosion, Manhattan" within seconds of the event.[5] People craved information quicker than the news could provide it.

> The elderly, as always, complain that the young do everything too fast

## ● Never say "know"

A fast market is a volatile market. In fact, the very definition of volatility is the kind of rapid turbulence certain markets encounter from time to time. We don't call changes that happen over decades volatile. Volatility used to be an exception. We used to think of most stocks, most markets and the majority of prices as fairly stable. When the

V-word was used, it was to characterize the anomaly – be it a certain time period, a certain commodity, a certain political situation and so forth. Volatility has become the norm nowadays. Never before have so many areas been characterized by rapid movements back and forth, up and down. This changes the assumption about stability as the norm, which in turn forces us to reconsider the very essence of knowledge. In a stable world, we can *know* things and we rest assured that the things we know will also be true tomorrow. In a volatile world, this is turned on its head. Yesterday's assumptions about countries, companies, people and prices are radically transformed, and just as we think we understand the new world, it changes shape yet again.

With this development, we need to change how we look at the world and what it is to *know* something. At film school, I read a book by the screenwriter William Goldman, who said that in Hollywood "nobody knows anything", a comment on the unpredictable nature of movies and movie-making. This is a good starting point for the unpredictable world we face. It turns out that there was a school called Black Mountain College of the Arts in the USA that had "never say know" as one of its operating principles.[6] These are great statements on a semantic level but very difficult for most people to apply on a daily basis. We need to make certain assumptions about the world around us if we are to function as human beings. What we need to develop is a greater level of imagination. Let's revisit the numerical sequence from earlier in the chapter:

$$2, 4, \ldots, \ldots$$

When I asked you what two numbers came next, I was looking for the logical, mathematically correct answer. Using another perspective, however, some equally correct answers could be 2, 4, 2, 4 or 2, 4, 36, 9 and so on. These are creative, imaginative answers that are based on criteria other than the strictly logical. They may be cumbersome in terms of the numerical sequence, but imagine if I asked you to design a telephone. Or to think about ways in which a city can protect itself against a terrorist attack. If you stick to logical answers in these cases, chances are that you would do quite a poor job. Imagination is vital in a volatile world where outcomes tend to be surprising, shocking, unexpected and very fast. This explains why many people were led astray into thinking that controlling risk – the probability of a certain outcome – was equivalent to controlling the unexpected.

**Imagination is vital in a volatile world**

## ● Tales of the unexpected

My grandmother – whose apartment I described earlier in the book – built a nest with my grandfather in the 1950s. Within ten years, they had three daughters, my mother being the oldest of three sisters. Since my grandfather was a pilot with SAS, the Scandinavian airline, they travelled extensively and lived in Rome for a few years. Their existence was on a trajectory that we could call "Family Life". My grandmother's idea of the future was most likely a scenario wherein she watched her kids grow up and spent lots of time travelling with my grandfather.

Then one day in 1965, when they were on the way home from a PTA meeting at school, their car skidded off the road and crashed, killing my grandfather instantly and leaving my grandmother in a coma. My mother, seventeen at the time, was forced to care for her younger sisters, and even though my grandmother eventually awoke from the coma, it took years before she could live without the assistance of some sort of hospital aid.

This story is not unique. Everyone encounters a number of unexpected incidents that end up changing their life – for better or worse – into something new. When it happens, it's painful. If you never imagined anything like this could ever happen, it's bound to be even more agonizing. The first law of economics states that "things that can't last forever won't". This is easy to forget, however, when you're

**The first law of economics states that "things that can't last forever won't"**

caught up in a surge of rational or irrational exuberance. Our brains are designed to be busy with the present, not confused by innumerable alternative scenarios.

That's what makes the majority of events and incidents that shape the modern world unexpected to a greater or lesser degree. Furthermore, when we invite imagination into the workplace and the individual becomes more powerful, you have a very powerful cocktail for unpredictability. Two guys inventing a world-changing search engine. Ten guys holding all of Mumbai hostage. Both were equally unexpected before they happened. That's why we need to develop what poet John Keats called a *negative capability* – "when a man is capable of being in uncertainties, mysteries, doubts, without any irritable reaching after fact and reason".[7]

## ● From money premium to time premium

Another change created by a faster society is the nature of status. Money used to be expensive and rare because most wealth was contained within rich families. Status is always dictated by scarce resources in society, and back then the word "luxury" was used to described things that reminded us of money. The best example of this is the human body. If you wanted to radiate power in the early 1900s, obesity was the way to go. In a world that had just faced starvation, showing off body fat was a sure means of conveying the message that you had the money to consume food excessively. You can still see this phenomenon in relatively poor countries. In richer countries, a combination of self-made wealth, significantly cheaper credit, mass-market production and so on has made money less exclusive than it once was. Fat and sugar, once rare and pricey commodities, are available on every street corner. In a millisecond world, where every moment counts, the increasingly dear resource is time. Yesterday's status symbol, obesity, is viewed as a disease and often attributed to poor diets and low incomes. The body we strive for today is lean, toned and tells other people that we spend some portion of our valuable time taking care of

**In a millisecond world, the increasingly dear resource is time**

our bodies. Showing off money is no longer a status symbol; rather, showing off time that you control yourself is.

Time status has been especially prevalent in the past decade. A luxury vacation has gone from being five days in an opulent hotel with chandeliers to barefoot luxury where solitude is to be savoured on a remote island, based on the principles of "authenticity", "simplicity" and other buzzwords. Wine is no longer just wine but a chance to show off knowledge – another sign of using time wisely – by adding a "did you know?" before you serve it. One of the most interesting examples is the rise of organic food. Most people who buy organic claim that they do it because of health or environmental reasons or both. In reality, few studies have conclusively proven that organic food is healthy or more benign to the environment in the long run. What we *do* know is that organic food is a lighter version of anthroposophist food. Anthroposophy is an "occult movement", according to its founder, and its way of harvesting the earth was filled with rituals and rules ("Only harvest in the light of the moon", and so on). Organic food production is a direct descendant of this kind of agricultural production, and its connection to time status is simple once you become aware of this connection. Letting things take their time and drawing attention to slow production characterize both anthroposophist and organic agriculture.

## ● Neophobia

Speed is one of the most frequently attacked phenomena of modern society. Our "race towards efficiency" is a "race to the bottom", many claim, pointing to the loss of handicrafts in favour of mass production or the mistreatment of animals and soil in industrial agriculture. Anti-speed movements like the Italian Città Slow and Slow Food have sprung up around the world to promote a slower lifestyle. Resistance to speed is nothing new. The belief that "things move too fast" was as prevalent in earlier centuries as it is today and will be tomorrow. Why? The most fundamental reason is that speed quickly changes the landscape in which we navigate and makes the previously familiar unfamiliar. The things we are allowed to get used to slowly are more likely to become accepted than the things we feel are thrust upon us. People have always been afraid of the unknown, and we tend to vehemently oppose the things we don't understand and the things we are afraid of. Homosexuality, fast food, digital gaming, file sharing, mass immigration and so on are features that are new, or less suppressed, in many societies today, but also phenomena that provoke knee-jerk reactions of outrage and disgust in many people. When things happen quickly, the forces of resistance tend to be stronger, since these things are seen as "unnatural".

> When things happen quickly, the forces of resistance tend to be stronger

## ● Don't extrapolate!

Whenever something new hits society's collective perception radar, many silly predictions are made about the future of this particular phenomenon. In the 1980s, with the rise of MTV, a massive resurgence of the musical was predicted. In the early 2000s, when the dotcom bubble burst, the death of all Web-based business was proclaimed. Most of these kinds of predictions tend to be wrong because they're based upon linear extrapolations of the present rather than imaginative scenarios of the future. Hype and bubble mentality are really just the extreme consequences of linear extrapolation: "Well, it's really big today so it's bound to be even bigger tomorrow." This is known as the gambler's fallacy, where you imagine patterns and order in randomness.

Every year around Christmas time, I'm phoned up by half a dozen journalists, all with the following question: "What do you foresee happening in the year ahead?" It is as predictable as it is unimaginative. To believe that you can view trends as an exercise in determinism is tantamount to witchcraft. A good trendspotter exists to uncover hidden truths, not gaze at some crystal ball. In a predictable world with, as academics are prone to say, "all else equal", we may have a decent chance of getting certain extrapolations of present data right. In reality, with speed creating a much more volatile landscape, we are far better off using our imagination and continually asking "what if?" to test new and provocative ideas.

Just as Marty McFly in *Back to the Future* started to change the future in the same moment that he began tampering with the past, so can we use insights and thoughts about the present to mould the future into something else. To quote a famous advertising executive: "We are so busy measuring public opinion that we forget we can mould it. We are also so busy listening to statistics we forget we can create them."[8]

# The Trendspotter Mission Manual

If you don't want to be caught off guard by a flock of black swans coming out of nowhere, here are some appropriate steps to take:

## CONSULT MORE PEOPLE!

THE WISDOM OF CROWDS WORKS SPLENDIDLY WHEN FANTASIZING ABOUT POTENTIAL OUTCOMES AND "WHAT IFS?" THIS WAS THE KEY INSIGHT OF THE POLICY ANALYSIS MARKET, PAM. THE PROJECT WAS PROPOSED AFTER 9/11 AND THE BASIC IDEA WAS TO PREDICT TERRORIST EVENTS THROUGH THE ONLINE SELLING OF "FUTURES".(9) THE IDEA IS CONTROVERSIAL AND THE US CONGRESS KILLED THE INITIATIVE BEFORE IT GOT OFF THE GROUND, BUT THAT DOESN'T STOP YOU AND ME FROM SETTING UP OUR OWN PAMS WHEN SPECULATING ABOUT THE FUTURE.

## INVEST IN SPEED!

FIND WAYS THAT WILL SHAVE OFF MINUTES AND SECONDS FROM ALL KINDS OF ACTIVITIES AND YOU WILL HAVE A COMPETITIVE ADVANTAGE IN LIFE AND BUSINESS.

## TRACK SCARCE RESOURCES!

BEING ABLE TO DETECT NEW STATUS SYMBOLS BEFORE OTHER PEOPLE DO IS A SUPERIOR, VALUABLE SKILL THAT YOU CAN SELL TO EVERYONE, FROM FASHION COMPANIES TO TRAVEL AGENTS TO PEOPLE LIKE ME.

## NEVER TRUST A ONE-WAY CURVE!

WHEN AN "EXPERT" POINTS TO A CURVE HEADING EITHER UP OR DOWN TO TELL YOU ABOUT THE FUTURE, BE SCEPTICAL! THAT CURVE HINGES ON SO MANY ASSUMPTIONS, IT IS BOUND TO BE WRONG. RECALL THE WISE WORDS OF ECONOMIST JOHN MAYNARD KEYNES: "THE INEVITABLE NEVER HAPPENS, THE UNEXPECTED ALWAYS DOES."

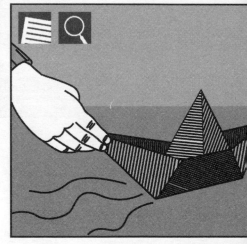

# 5 Beyond the horizon

## How an older society means a lot more than grey hair

*All science fiction writers, whether they admit it or not, are writing metaphorically about the present. To extrapolate the future is really to comment on the now ... The job of a science fiction writer, historically, has been to understand how technology and social factors interact.*

– Cory Doctorow

## ● "Meet George Jetson!"

George has a beautiful wife, Jane, and two kids, Elroy and Judy. He has a job and a comfortable middle-class life. By the way, George lives in the future.

He drives his family in a fold-up spaceship. Elroy attends Little Dipper School, a free-floating hovering platform, and is dropped off in a little glass bubblepod shot out from the family spaceship. Judy studies at Orbit High School, another hovercraft. Jane goes shopping at the spacemall after taking George's wallet with her. He gets slightly annoyed. But what can you do about women?

George arrives at work, folds his spacecraft up into a briefcase and takes the horizontal conveyor belt – the people mover – to work. Once there, he puts his feet up on the desk and dozes off. The future does indeed look bright. At least for white middle-class men.

The Jetsons were featured in a *Flintstones*-like cartoon broadcast in the late 1960s and set in the not-too-distant future, when we all supposedly drove spaceships, lived in or near space and surrounded ourselves with space-age gizmos like nuclear ovens and teleportation machines. There is just one small problem with the future scenario portrayed in *The Jetsons*: it looks more like the 1960s updated with new gadgets than the actual 2000s. The families shown were always demographic clichés with a heterosexual couple and two kids. There were no single households or same-sex marriages in *The Jetsons*. Jane Jetson had no job and spent her days cleaning the house or shopping, spending George's money. Female emancipation – arguably one of the most important forces since the 1960s, when *The Jetsons* was first broadcast – is notably absent. Finally, who in their right mind goes to work and falls asleep in the 2000s – the era of downsizing, outsourcing, profit-sharing and management by objectives?

What the cartoon's creators had failed to take into account, knowingly or not, were the invisible trends behind the gadgets and gimmicks which would ultimately have a much greater impact on the future than spaceships and hovering high schools.

It's hard to blame anyone for failing to see the invisible. Our lens is broken and there's very little we can do about that. More troubling is that we continually see the world as technology-centric, believing that technological inventions and machines are what ultimately drive the world forward. We tend to overestimate the effects of nanotechnology and the Internet and underestimate the role that human emotions and values play in shaping the society of the future. In addition, we often suffer from Presentism. This syndrome sets in when we overestimate the impact of the present on the future. We think that tomorrow will be more or less like today. Examples include the belief in the 1960s that Brazil was one of the world's future superpowers; the belief in the 1970s in free energy from nuclear power plants; the belief in the 1980s that stock markets would only surge upwards; and the belief in the 1990s that the entire world would become one big dotcom colony. Some of these predictions may have been wrong only in terms of timing – who's to say that we won't live in an all-Brazilian cyberspace fuelled by free energy sources and eternal wealth some time in the future? Nevertheless, predictions like these are usually created by over-extrapolating from present conditions and failing to imagine new developments and invisible trends underneath and beyond media headlines.

> **We tend to overestimate the effects of nanotechnology and the Internet**

## ● Old men in beards

Whenever movies try to portray old age, out come the wrinkle prosthetics, the white hair wig and the long white beard. This is the stereotypical image of old age, and if the formula was broken – if a
90-year-old man was portrayed with bulging muscles or no wrin-
kles – we would have a hard time understanding what was going
on and what the film-makers were trying to tell us. This is important to note, since current research suggests that, through healthier
lifestyles, replacement surgery and other medical breakthroughs,
human lifespans will increase drastically, just as they have already
over the past few centuries. This may not imply that a 90-year-old
will look like a Hollywood hunk, but it means that several things
about what it means to be "old" will change. First, 70 years of age
won't be "old" any more, just as 47, the average lifespan in 1850, and
thus "old age", isn't considered particularly "old" today.[1] Second, life
and society will change drastically to adapt to a population whose
lives have just exploded with new opportunities. Just as divorces,
multiple careers and Viagra are signs today of an older population
with plenty of mileage to go, the future will bring as yet unseen and
surprising changes to cater to the "Hundred-Plus-ers".

## ● Now is later

When my wife and I had twin boys in early 2008, we were delighted
and devastated. Delighted because having children is truly a miracle,
and devastated because life as we had known it was over and the new
existence consisted of sleepless nights and nappy changes. The interesting aspect of this, however, is that neither of us thought that the
situation would ever change. We thought that nights would be sleepless and nappies would be changed *for the rest of our lives*. We were
thoroughly unable to see beyond the horizon of today, as if our children would be babies for ever. This is a signifying trait of the human

brain. It's built primarily to deal with the here and now, which is why a "sixth sense" remains a fantasy and the other five senses are designed to detect things in our nearest spatial and time-based surroundings. This might cause heartache for the teenager whose girlfriend just broke up with him – "I'll never find someone like her!" – or for the young parents who think their sons will still be drinking formula at their wedding reception. More seriously, being locked into present patterns of thought constitutes a giant obstacle against planning for the future, especially on the kind of scale that society and markets rely on. How do you explain a city to someone who knows only villages? How do you explain MP3 technology to someone who didn't even know that music could be recorded? How do you explain air travel to someone who hasn't even seen a car?

How do you explain a city to someone who knows only villages?

## ● The Jetsons revisited

George, Jane, Elroy and Judy Jetson were figments of an imagination stuck in the 1960s. Had the programme introduced such progressive thoughts as downsizing or female emancipation, it would have been unable to communicate with a mass audience, so the series' creators extrapolated present conditions into a futurist version of the 1960s. We do the same thing today when we hear that "populations are getting older", and we envision cities full of Zimmer frames, wheelchairs and people who resemble our grandparents. We use our current perception of old age instead of focusing on the many unseen, underlying societal changes that are a lot more impactful when it comes to an ageing society.

Social scientists often point to *development blocks*. These are related areas that develop in unison. A simple example is the connection between architecture and music, whereby a new type of building technology creates a new type of concert hall, which in turn enables a new type of resonance and a new kind of music to be played. Statisticians call this *multivariate analysis*, whereby several different variables change at the same time. Had *The Jetsons'* creators taken multivariate analysis into account, they would have seen how female emancipation, technological development, inflation-reducing measures, stock markets and corporate strategists were conspiring to create the kind of society we see today.

Successful marketers exploit this inability of the human mind to understand changes in many dimensions. That's why they still insist on calling fancy, mobile handsets "mobile telephones", even though they could have been called "mobile computers" or just given a new name that made no specific reference to the mobile nature of the device. Marketers call these references to familiar phenomena "handrails" – mental frameworks that help customers understand what a new product or service is or does: a *mobile* telephone, *healthier* bread, *online* travel agencies and so on. Innovation history is full of anecdotes about how pioneers of new technologies failed to take the full impact of a new technology into account. Alexander Graham Bell famously thought the telephone to be ideal to transmit symphonic music long distance, to use one of many examples.

## The many unseen dimensions of an ageing society

Human ageing is the result of conspiring biological forces in our bodies: internal processes slow down and become less efficient. External wear and tear takes its toll on body organs. The body becomes less and less adept at healing and adapting. It's almost as if the body is on a timer programmed to kill off the person at some specific point in time. As we all know, however, this timer can be tweaked by using a combination of diet, lifestyle, medicine, replacement surgery and so on. There are even scientists who argue that ageing is an engineering flaw and that we can actually cure it, thereby prolonging human life by many, many decades. We can see in our rear-view mirror that longevity has increased drastically in the past century.

Fifty used to be considered old. That was a "natural" time to die. If you die at fifty today, your death is considered premature. Eighty-five is a more "natural" time to depart earthly life today. The word "natural", as we can see, has nothing to do with nature's plans for us but is merely a statistical reference to the most frequent occurrence. It is therefore likely that a death at age 85 will be considered premature in the coming century and that 130 might turn out to be a more "natural" age at which to die. The rate at which our lifespan increases – on average – is around five hours every day.[2] Every day, five hours are tagged on at the end of our collective longevity. The cumulative effect of these five daily hours is profound and entails a lot more than a stereotypical view of old people.

> There are scientists who argue that ageing is an engineering flaw and that we can cure it

At the heart of the matter is the fact that with increased time on earth comes an increase in the number of choices a human being can make in a lifetime. Hence, divorce can be attributed both to a secularization of society and to the fact that a lifelong marriage is less feasible in a world where you will need to stay together a lot longer than you did a few centuries ago, when matrimony was invented.

> With increased time on earth comes an increase in the number of choices a human being can make in a lifetime

Another impact old age has is on our careers. In a previous chapter, I wrote about how industries and sectors are fragmenting. The same thing is happening to jobs. The profession of a car mechanic, for instance, has fragmented into more than ten different roles as automobiles have grown increasingly complex. Furthermore, we are free to invent our own jobs today in a way that is unparalleled historically. The resulting situation is one of virtually limitless choice when it comes to jobs and careers.

Let's add a longer life into the equation and see what happens. If we go back a century or so, the number of jobs available was more limited. Assume – for the sake of simplicity – that there were five jobs available to a person back then. These could have been soldier, writer, ironmonger, farmer and academic, to name five random examples. Since life was shorter, we were able to try out a maximum of two jobs long enough to consider them a career. Remember, the time span and the number of choices are simplifications. Using the concept of permutations – the number of possible combinations within a larger group; in this case two potential careers available within a pool of five potential occupations – we see that there are 25 possibilities available. The implication is that there were only 25 different kinds of individuals, from a career perspective. There were soldiers who became writers, ironmongers who became academics, farmers who became soldiers, and so on. The specific numbers do not matter much for this exercise. What is striking is how this figure explodes when we add more years to our lifespan and expand the number of possible jobs. Let us assume – again in a simplified example – that people today have an average of 45 possible occupations to choose from. We can become spa therapists, Java programmers, social workers, DJs or trendspotters as well as farmers, academics, writers, soldiers and ironmongers, of course. Our careers are a lot longer now so we can assume that a person might have up to ten different jobs in his or her lifetime. This simple example, using permutations, creates nearly three quadrillion* possibilities. There are, in other words, significantly more job permutations than there are people on earth. The implication of this is that, as we grow older, we naturally drift towards a greater degree of uniqueness between people.

---

* Quadrillion = seventeen zeros.

## ● Younique

To claim that we become more unique is inaccurate. We are designed in a unique way. The combination of adenine, guanine, cytosine and thymine that constitutes our DNA differs between individuals by about 0.5 per cent.[3] To put this figure in context, it means that for two days every year, every single living human being does something, feels something and thinks in a way that is unique to him or her. We can call this our "two days of uniqueness", and they tend to be spread out in seconds and minutes across a year for most people. Societies have up until the past decades favoured collective action, with the result being that differences between people have been ironed out, at least when it comes to jobs and professions. At the dawn of industrial production, seeing people as clones and cogs was the very essence of efficient production. Intelligence and creativity were seen as anomalies that rewarded only some higher beings in society.

With people living longer and capitalism refined into MyCapital, we see people becoming more and more specialized. The salesman becomes a physiotherapist and a gardener. The taxi driver becomes a writer and adventurer. The probability that two people will, over time, choose exactly the same path is minuscule. Like statues chiselled out of a giant block, we are honed over time into people with unique skills and experiences. We follow the "fate" programmed by our DNA. This argument would have made a nice self-help book if it weren't for the fact that there is high economic value in uniqueness and specialization. People who embrace their own uniqueness can earn more from what they do than people who don't. It's elementary. Scarcity is rewarded with a price premium in economics. Unique skills are more sought after than commoditized, rudimentary abilities. What makes me optimistic is that every single human being, through the simple act of living and working, is – consciously or not – gathering a set of unique skills over time. Take myself as an example. I am the only living trendspotting business school/film school graduate who has sold cat litter and lottery tickets, worked in an advertising agency and written a (failed) novel. My experience enables me to have unique ideas, and it is these ideas that I sell. Ideas, as we all know, are the most valuable currency in the world today and, to use a famous quote, "the greatest ideas you will ever get are the ones that other people don't understand". These are the kinds of ideas that fewer people can copy or steal and that few other people have envisioned before you did.

> The greatest ideas you will ever get are the ones that other people don't understand

## ● A life less ordinary

Neophobics often wonder what the use of living longer is. Isn't it practical and natural to die around ninety, as we do now? This assumption contains two fallacies. First, history has shown us that the "natural" time of death is highly flexible. Second, it's only practical to have people die off if we see the workplace as a finite pool of opportunity which the labour force enters and exits. If, on the other hand, we view work as a flexible arena that can expand continuously into unknown territories, then each of us will have something new to bring into it. It has been said that whereas Western societies grieve at the death of a child for all he or she never had the chance to experience, many other cultures grieve at the death of an elder because of all the unique knowledge that has been lost with him or her. What I have argued in this chapter is that longer life opens up a new unseen dimension in life and in business. Increased longevity gives us more time to sample different careers and experiences, with the end result being a workforce that is more diverse and specialized than ever. This is an abstract idea to get across. We cannot see people's skills or ideas. Science fiction movies would have to present each character with a business card for us to understand that "this character has some really unique dimensions". It's more convenient to bring out the prosthetics and the wig, so the chances are that people will continue to envision "an older population" as a giant congregation of silver-haired people and miss the bigger picture completely.

# The Trendspotter Mission Manual

This is a chapter about taking multiple factors into account when analysing the future. Here are some examples of what you can do to avoid the *Jetsons* fallacies:

TECHNOLOGY NEEDS TO BECOME BORING TO CHANGE SOCIETY!
DON'T RAVE ABOUT NEW INVENTIONS. TRY TO ENVISION HOW SOCIETY IS CHANGING AND HOW WE MIGHT EVENTUALLY USE THIS PARTICULAR TECHNOLOGY. REMEMBER THAT IT TOOK THE AEROPLANE ALMOST HALF A CENTURY TO BECOME CHEAP ENOUGH FOR ANYONE TO FLY.

DON'T TAKE ANYTHING FOR GRANTED!
TAKE NEWSPAPERS, FOR EXAMPLE. MEDIA ANALYST CLAY SHIRKY STATES THAT: "THEY WERE SEEN AS SUCH A GOOD IDEA FOR SUCH A LONG TIME THAT PEOPLE FELT THE NEWSPAPER BUSINESS MODEL WAS PART OF A DEEP TRUTH ABOUT THE WORLD, RATHER THAN JUST THE WAY THINGS HAPPENED TO BE. IT'S LIKE THE FALL OF COMMUNISM, WHERE A LOT OF THE EASTERN EUROPEAN SATELLITE STATES HAD AN EASIER TIME BECAUSE THERE WERE STILL PEOPLE ALIVE WHO REMEMBERED LIFE BEFORE THE SOVIET UNION NOBODY IN RUSSIA REMEMBERED IT. NEWSPAPER PEOPLE ARE LIKE RUSSIANS, IN A WAY."(4)

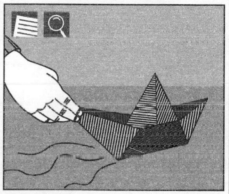

STUDY THE BIGGER PICTURE!
WHAT TRAJECTORY IS SOCIETY ON? LINEAR TRENDS MAY INDEED BE DECEPTIVE, BUT LONG-TERM DEVELOPMENTS MIGHT UNCOVER HIDDEN TRUTHS ABOUT THE WORLD WE LIVE IN. THINGS THAT WE TAKE FOR GRANTED AND DON'T CONSIDER PART OF A LARGER CHANGE.

LOOK BACK AT LEAST AS FAR AS YOU'RE LOOKING FORWARD!
THIS ADVICE, FROM INSTITUTE FOR THE FUTURE'S PAUL SAFFO, IS VITAL WHEN IT COMES TO SPECULATING ABOUT A FUTURE SOCIETY.

## Extended Mission Manual – three lessons in how to be unique

We cannot *become* unique. We can only embrace the fact that we *are* unique by about 0.5 per cent. This is an important distinction, and it's also what saves this book from the "how to" category. My thoughts in this section should, nevertheless, be taken with a pinch of salt, since they are personal observations rather than dogmatic rules.

The first lesson I learned in staying unique is to avoid any kind of trap whereby you imitate others – explicitly or not. A couple of years ago, I entered a lookalike contest in a tabloid magazine. It's not something I usually do, and that's why the memory of this questionable activity stands out in my mind as a strong learning experience. In the photo I sent in, I claimed to look like a well-known actor, and many of my friends agreed with me. More surprisingly, the tabloid agreed with me. This is a transcript of their phone call congratulating me on winning (!) the lookalike contest.

**Tabloid journalist:** *Magnus, you've won our lookalike contest!*

**Me:** *Wow, thanks!*

**Tabloid journalist:** *Your photo bore an uncanny resemblance to [Actor X].*

**Me:** *I'm glad you think so.*

**Tabloid journalist:** *There is, unfortunately, a catch …*

**Me:** *Oh?*

**Tabloid journalist:** *Yes, well, you see … first prize is a trip to Stockholm and you already live there, right?*

**Me:** *Right.*

**Tabloid journalist:** *So we decided to award the prize to this young guy from Gothenburg who has never been to Stockholm … His photo* *isn't as good as yours but he* needs *this prize more than you do.*

**Me:** ... (stunned silence)

The lesson in this story is that when we imitate other people, mediocrity gets rewarded. The question "How come she gets a higher salary than I do when I work so much harder than her" is futile. When we define ourselves by trying to look or be like somebody else, we are doomed to fail. That is the first lesson in being unique.

The second lesson is as simple as is it difficult. Everybody has heard the cliché that we are born as originals but die as clones. This is manifested in how our wishes for birthday presents change over time. Ask a five-year-old what he or she wants for their birthday and their eyes light up: "The doll I saw last week, the gadget on TV, a spaceship, my own beach, being a cowboy for a day ..." and so on. When an adult gets asked the same question, he or she will merely sigh and say something along the lines of : "Well, I guess a book would be nice ... or a new spatula ... or some time for myself." Somewhere along the line, our enthusiasm, our dreams and our ability to wish

> **The test of a first-rate intelligence is the ability to hold two opposed ideas in the mind at the same time**

for bigger and better things got lost. The birthday wish is an excellent opportunity to hone the skills of having bigger dreams, since everyone gets an annual practice session. Besides, we always talk about how giving to others makes us happy, so when we become better at dreaming and wishing, we will most likely make people in our vicinity happier. Talk about a win-win situation.

The third and final lesson has to do with the rules of attraction. What attracts people to other people or to certain phenomena? This question doesn't have one single answer, but I found an interesting clue in a book a few years ago.[5] It talked about why certain products – in this case coffee or ice cream – generated nearly fanatical consumers. The quick and easy answer would probably focus on the caffeine or the sugar, but the book's explanation went deeper. It claimed that coffee and ice cream contain an inherent paradox and that it is this "broken soul" which drives people mad with desire. Coffee contains caffeine, which creates stimulation, but it is also closely connected with having a break, enabling us to relax. Stimulation and relaxation constitute a paradox that only coffee can deliver. This is known as a "paradessence" – a paradoxical essence. F. Scott Fitzgerald once said that "The test of a first-rate intelligence is the ability to hold two opposed ideas in the mind at the same time, and still retain the ability to function."

Once you start searching for paradessence, you start detecting it everywhere. Punk rock was once described as making "ugliness beautiful". John Lennon's attraction was attributed to the fact that he was both masculine and feminine at the same time. When people are asked to describe what attracted them to their partners, they often focus on a paradessence: "I saw the boy inside the man" or "She has a kind of sexy innocence about her". Ice cream is probably the most Freudian of them all. It's highly connected to the innocence of childhood but is consumed by licking and sucking: innocence and eroticism in the same product. What we need to do to be unique is to define and continuously sharpen our paradessence. What two paradoxical directions are inherent in our personality? This stands in sharp contrast to how most people describe themselves in résumés or job interviews, where only one side of the personality is emphasized: "I'm diligent, hard working, analytical, curious and outgoing."

# 6 Missing the bigger picture

How a new perspective is the world's most valuable currency

*To a worm in an apple, the world is made of apple.*

– Unknown

# All business-class travellers are idiots

Flying has lost its lustre in the past few decades. What was once glamorous and romantic has been reduced to standing in line, taking your shoes off and pouring out any excess liquids at security control before proceeding to an overcrowded terminal building and aircraft. The one and only benefit of being so close to many people is the opportunity it gives trendspotters to study the travel habits, onboard behaviour and duty-free shopping habits of fellow travellers.

There is another way to travel if you're willing to drastically increase your expenditure. Business class is designed to shield you from the queues and the hustle of economy class. The check-in area is secluded and quick. Security is handled in a "fast-track" section, designed, as the name suggests, to make the procedure swift. Instead of lingering in the duty-free shops or newsagents, the business class travellers usually hang out in "The Lounge", a members-only VIP section where newspapers and snacks are free. Once aboard the plane, these people congregate at the front in seats that are strategically spaced out to maximize comfort and minimize contact with other passengers. Glamorous as it may be, it is also secluded from the real world. Business class is an appropriate name. The busy class. The people who are too busy to loiter in the real world. Or the *other* world, at least. Business-class travellers become idiots in the original Latin meaning of the word – alone.

**Business class is a metaphor for how most people live their life**

Business class is a metaphor for how most people live their life. We are content in our sphere of the world and oblivious to the many other worlds that we miss. Travel – whether as an intellectual or a geographic endeavour – may open our minds to some extent, but it is merely a temporary refuge from the imprisoning convenience of our immediate realm. This chapter will deal with some of the different ways in which a myopic view of the world blinds us.

## ● Blind to blindness

"Everyone wants to believe that they have good taste and a good sense of humour." These are the words of Meg Ryan's Sally in the movie *When Harry Met Sally*. We can add to this that everyone wants to believe that the worldview they have is true. That is the deal struck between the brain and the eyes. The brain may fantasize as long as what the eyes see is considered superior to fantasies and daydreams in the hierarchy of consciousness. Even if the eyes never lie, perspective does. A personal example of this comes from when I worked for an automotive brand a few years ago, tasked with repositioning their luxury brand for the European market. The brief the marketing director had given me stated that the luxury brand – call it "Brand X" – had experienced huge problems in gaining market share and lingered somewhere on the fringes of the luxury car market. Armed with this insight, I set about conducting my own analysis. My finding was that the marketing director must have been mistaken. The car was everywhere. I saw it parked on street corners, in traffic jams, in garages, in magazines, and so on. What I had forgotten was that my perspective blinded me. First because I lived in an affluent part of Stockholm where the car was over-represented, and second because my perception was switched to a selective mode, in which I was on the lookout for this particular brand. When I made new observations – this time comparing the number of sightings of Brand X to those of other luxury car brands – I realized that there was indeed a problem. Perspective and perception had dulled my senses in the first instance.

## The perils of perspective

There are a number of famous quotes describing the impact of perspective change. "Human perspective is worth 80 IQ points,"[1] for example, or the more famous "The mind, once expanded by a new idea, never regains its original dimensions."[2] In fact, belief in some kind of omnipresent higher being can be seen as a manifestation of our collective desire to be everywhere all the time. Apart from the general laws of physics working against us, there are two other innate forces that severely limit our perspective. The first is our need for predictability. We prefer most things in our life to be more or less anticipated. Even if we consider ourselves to be the adventurous type, we hope that certain universal laws will always apply. A rock should fall down when dropped, for example. The person to whom you were married as you went to bed last night should still be your wife when you wake up. Smiling at a stranger in the street should not be interpreted as hostile, and so on. People lacking this dimension in their life – call it *everydayness* – are most likely suffering from a severe mental impairment and condemned to a life of fear and misery. The downside of everydayness, however, is that we seldom open ourselves to new impressions and we remain stuck on a carousel of daily routine.

> We prefer most things in our life to be more or less anticipated

The second obstruction to new perspectives is the company we keep. When asked, most people will describe their own circle of friends and acquaintances as highly diverse. We tend to look at fairly superficial attributes such as nationality, looks and occupation and draw the erroneous conclusion that these people represent a fair and balanced cross-section of society at large. What we fail to take into account is *homophily*, whereby we tend to be drawn to people who resemble us in some way. Your friends may indeed have varying incomes and educational backgrounds, yet their values, ways of thinking and general outlook will closely match yours. This is an invisible force we tend not to consider. We just like certain people because we like them. A closer look would reveal the reason why we like many of these people is because they seem to understand and appreciate us in some deeper manner. They laugh at our jokes. They have solutions for our problems. They like doing the same things as us. Many of us assume that connecting to the Internet is an antidote to homophily since it connects us to a wider world. Yet World Wide Web usage is not evenly distributed around the world. The online population is a skewed sample of the global population. The median Internet user is a young, well-educated man in proximity to a large city. This is reflected in, among other things, the year-end surveys of search engines, where the most searched words annually usually end up being some kind of celebrity, as well as entries for various illegal file-sharing and bit torrent sites. The median global inhabitant is a poor woman living in the vicinity of a war zone, so Paris Hilton or YouTube would probably not be her first priorities were she to wander into cyberspace any time soon.

> **The online population is a skewed sample of the global population**

## ● The pitfalls of perception

When Richard Dawkins, one of the world's greatest scientists, was asked what question he'd most like answered, he responded that he would above all else like to know what human consciousness is; what happens in the brain when we are conscious? Human perception is, in other words, one of the great mysteries of our time. We are aware of some its limitations, though. In a previous chapter, I described "Spousal Obstruction Syndrome", whereby our view of the world is clouded by things that tug at our emotional strings, such as our families. This limits our view of the world since it creates a mental microcosm that bears little or no resemblance to the world outside. To quote the Talmud, "We see things not as *they* are but as *we* are."

There are a number of other ways in which our perception can wreak havoc on our ability to spot trends even more efficiently than business class travel can. These can be divided into three groups: the tendency to see patterns where none exist; the tendency to seek confirmatory evidence; and the use of preconceived biases. The underlying cause of all three groups is one and the same: convenience. Preconceived biases, the mental rules known as heuristics, are mental short cuts intended to save valuable brain resources. It's more convenient to assume that someone who looks like a woman is a woman rather than a transvestite. Seeking confirmatory evidence is the very nature of markets. When we have bought something or made a decision, we want to know that we made the right decision. When people disagree in boardrooms, they usually introduce themselves as "playing devil's advocate", which is indicative of how reluctant many of us are to scrutinize decisions or hypotheses. Rather than just stating that we'll use common sense and scrutinize the information given, we

> Weaving events together is seductive because it makes chaos and complexity seem structured

claim to be playing some sort of game in which we assume the role of a hellish being. Finally, pattern recognition is one of the most fundamental building blocks of human perception. We splice together bits and pieces into a coherent view. Think about media coverage, for instance. Whenever something happens which stirs our emotions, media outlets go to great lengths to find parallels. One terrorist attack must mean more are on the way. One bank collapse must be connected to other economic mayhem, and so on. Weaving these events together is seductive because it makes chaos and complexity seem structured and ordered. It's like playing Tetris, where each building block is a news story that just has to fit together with other news stories somehow. This way of grouping information usually proves misleading.

## ● Everything all the time

At a dinner party a few years ago, I was introduced to a dance show producer. The man was a middle-aged, flamboyant entrepreneur who had recently introduced so-called "street dancing" into Sweden. This particular genre has Afro-American urban roots and is characterized by its blend of break-dancing and acrobatics. When he found out that I was a trendspotter, he exclaimed: "Dancing is a strong trend right now!" I smiled, nodded and we kept talking about trends, dancing and life in general. For some time afterwards, however, I kept thinking about what he had said about dancing being a trend. It seemed wrong somehow. Dancing had never gone away. It had been there all the time in different shapes. From the swing dance of the 1950s to the jitterbug, punk pogoing, electric boogie, Michael Jackson's Moonwalk, *Dirty Dancing*, ballroom dancing, *Dancing with the Stars*, and so on. How can dancing be a trend – an indicator of change – if it never went away?

The answer is twofold. First, for this particular producer, the form of dance that he represents was new to many people at the time. Second, the mass-medial lens that we often refer to as the mainstream has continually increased and decreased its focus on dancing over the years, just as other phenomena drift in and out of its view. This was a time when its focus on dancing was increasing. Media play a leading role as cultivators of trends in society. Many things labelled "trends" are merely phenomena that have been around for years and have only recently been elevated into view by larger media outlets such as national TV channels or newspapers. Climate change, organic food, Islamic fundamentalism, healthy eating and digital file sharing are just some of the many examples of issues and debates that loitered for years on the fringes of society before they hit the big time of op-ed pages and headline news.

As a matter of fact, studying the fringes of societal debates is a useful indicator in predicting what will be considered a "trend" in the coming months and years. Lazy journalists are the driving force. The idealistic notion of a journalist as a passionate truth-seeker pursuing stories in the trenches is belied by a reality where many journalists merely copy and rewrite stories found in smaller niche media. The music editor of a national newspaper will scour music blogs and fanzines for "the next big thing". The political pundit will scrutinize the debates of smaller, more extreme magazines. And so on. Medial fragmentization, of the kind that we've experienced in the past decade, means that the opportunity to "discover" things is greater than ever. The collective window of consciousness previously referred to as "the mainstream" is getting smaller, and a fragmented arena of mainstreams is emerging.

The implication is that the word "trend" will take on a drastically new meaning. It used to mean "an emerging phenomenon in the mass-medial lens". Increasingly, however, virtually anything can be described as a trend since virtually anything can be defined as new to some group of people

**Virtually anything can be defined as new to some group of people in the world**

in the world. Take the song "Torn", for example, written by Scott Cutler, Anne Preven and Phil Thornalley. The song is best known in its 1997 reincarnation, sung by Australian soap opera actress Natalie Imbruglia, yet it had been released by different artists, including a group featuring the song's writers, at least three times before this, starting with a Danish version in 1993. The same idea rerecorded until it hit the mainstream music scene.

We can see similar developments everywhere we look. The piece of technology that had been around for years but became ubiquitous when a large technological brand adopted it. The findings of a forgotten scientist given new life by a popular science writer. Gaining a larger audience – whether as a song, a hypothesis or a technology – is the result of a number of different factors, including timing, marketing, product refinement and distribution. Surprisingly often, it's not the "best" idea which becomes the most popular. Natalie Imbruglia's way of singing "Torn", for example, has been described by one of the song's writers as "lobotomized".[3] Things need to be simplified, sexed up and made aesthetically accessible if they are to gain large audiences. That's why many people feel betrayed when "their" band or author makes it big, since the artist had to sacrifice some aspect of their product or personality in the transition from smaller to larger venues or readership.

## ● Eternal trends

As the word "trend" became increasingly popular in the early 2000s thanks in part to the information abundance created by the Internet, the amount of hogwash passed off as "trend reports" increased rapidly. One of the biggest contributing factors to lowering the standards of trendspotting was the tendency to present everyday phenomena as something new and revolutionary. A number of examples included:

● *Health and convenience*: In an area reborn as "wellness" and "ease of mind" in the early 2000s, the reports focusing on healthy eating and the streamlining of everyday activities failed to realize that these have been the strongest drivers throughout human history. The story of science is ultimately a story about man's quest to make life a little easier and longer.

● *Self-expression*: A plethora of reports and seminars between 2000 and 2007 focused on how "the young of today want to get noticed". How exactly does that differ from any other generation in the history of mankind? The answer is that it doesn't. To be human is to want to leave a mark somehow, somewhere. From cave paintings and monuments to YouTube videos, the urge to take something from within you – a piece of knowledge, a moment of inspiration, an insight, an idea – and put into somebody else can be seen throughout history and not just in Generations X, Y or Z.

- *Impressions and experiences*: Countless reports and newspaper articles keep on using hyperbolic statements like "sensual stimulus overload" or "our urge for ever larger spectacles" as if these things are signs of the times we live in. They are not. Human senses have continually adapted to new surroundings, whether it's the nose blocking out the smell of charred coal in the eighteenth century or the eyes ignoring a new digital billboard in the twentieth. Equally eternal is our quest to cut through the clutter and capture people's attention, whether through young boys yelling out the current news headlines to sell newspapers or a ridiculously expensive special-effects movie designed to outshine what has come before it. Spectacle is an eternal human desire, from early carnivals and theatre pieces to present-day rock concerts and flash mobs.

> The story of science is ultimately a story about man's quest to make life easier and longer

- *Technology*: We have seen many attempts to find a suitable name that will neatly summarize our age, just as we imagine "The Iron Age" captures a specific period thousands of years ago. These efforts usually incorporate the words "oil" or "network" or "nano", or simply settle for "The Age of Technology". When the word "technology" is uttered, most people make the mistake of assuming that it refers to something new and electronic. As a matter of fact, technology is the description of the process whereby mankind has continually learned to tame new materials and processes for his own benefit. Corrugated iron, asphalt, sailing and alcohol are just as valid examples of technology as nanotubes, computer software and hybrid engines. What's more surprising, however, is that technology acts a lot like energy, in that it never really disappears. From steam engines still available to buy on eBay to ancient principles of physics applied in a new building material, technology is continually transferred and transformed into new shapes without disappearing.

Using "eternal" and "trend" in the same sentence seems oxymoronic. Yet we can see in all these instances that there is indeed something eternal about things that have been described as "trends" in the past decade. A way of clarifying this is to use a metaphor. Think of trends as a tree, where the foliage is the short-term manifestation and the branches and trunk the long-term changes. Ayurvedic massage and organic food are the current manifestations (the leaves) of man's eternal quest for health (the trunk). Cirque du Soleil, Imax and Shakespeare's Globe Theatre are present reincarnations of our eternal need for spectacle. The white earpieces of your MP3 player are the modern-day equivalent of an eighteenth-century powdered wig – a symbol of belonging.

## ● This is my truth, tell me yours ...

In the 1960s, a number of professional opinion-makers – predominantly fashion journalists and social commentators – had noticed that hat usage had declined, even disappeared completely within some groups. The hat had for a long time been a must in any male wardrobe and now it was just gone. What had happened? The opinion-makers jostled for position to deliver the right answer. Surely the fact that JFK was not wearing a hat at his inauguration had something to do with it. The rebelliousness of youth was the culprit. Hat manufacturers had fallen behind other fashion manufacturers in terms of style and colour. And so on. What's interesting is that most of these commentators completely missed the fact that hat usage had been on the wane for decades, not just for a few years in the 1960s.[4] Yet the declining trend had to slip below some critical threshold for these people to notice. The long-term trend was described as a short-term fashion issue. The reasons behind declining hat usage had to do with more complex shifts from an agricultural economy to an industrial one, as well as social conditioning. In the early 1900s, people had just emerged from an agricultural society in which hats were a protection against the elements, and the path in life that people were expected to take mimicked that of their parents, so the hat was picked up as a fashion statement by the next generation too. Within a few decades, however, following in your father's footsteps was out of fashion and suburbanization meant that people spent a lot more time in cars – an impractical place for a hat. When we limit our perspective in time and place, we miss these long-term, complex yet important variables that shape our everyday lives.

The question, then, is how we can break out of the shackles labelled "here and now". The right answer is that we can't. The human brain has evolved to stay in the present, along with our body. Yet we can make efforts to limit the blind spots of these biological prerequisites.

Toyota, the car manufacturer, has a core value that they instil in their employees which you and I can also benefit from. It's called *"Genchi Genbutsu"*, which translates roughly as "go to the source" – don't just trust second-hand information but make an effort to see things with your own eyes. In a world where secondary information is abundant, this idea becomes increasingly useful and important. It's a call to arms for us to get up from our desk or our couch and go out into the world to see things from new vantage points. It may be inconvenient and risky, but that's the price we have to pay if we want a worldview that is bigger than the diameter of our skull. *Immersive* trendspotting as opposed to merely passive trendspotting.

# The Trendspotter Mission Manual

If you want to master immersive trendspotting, here is what you need to do:

PRACTISE XENOPHILIA!
TALK TO STRANGERS. IT'S INCONVENIENT AND A LITTLE SCARY BUT IT FORCES YOU TO ENGAGE WITH A WORLD OUTSIDE YOUR OWN. I KNOW OF A TRENDSPOTTER WHOSE ENTIRE METHODOLOGY WAS ASKING STRANGERS IN AIRPORTS THE QUESTION "ARE YOU HAPPY?"

MAKE TIME FOR GENCHI GENBUTSU REALITY CHECKS!
WE ARE DROWNING IN SECONDARY INFORMATION – REPORTS, E-MAILS, MAGAZINES, WEBSITES – AND HAVE LESS TIME THAN EVER TO SEE THE WORLD WITH OUR OWN EYES. BLOCK OFF DAYS, EVEN WEEKS, IN WHICH TO DO THIS. IT WILL GIVE YOU INVALUABLE INSIGHTS.

USE PUBLIC TRANSPORT!
GO TO WHERE THE PEOPLE ARE. DON'T SPEND ALL YOUR TIME IN TAXIS AND BUSINESS-CLASS LOUNGES.

BE SCEPTICAL OF THE WORDS "LATEST TREND".
MOST THINGS WE SEE AND DO ARE MERELY REINCARNATIONS OF EARLIER VERSIONS. TRY TO FIND HISTORICAL EQUIVALENTS OF PRESENT PHENOMENA. THERE ARE BOUND TO BE A NUMBER OF THEM.

ASK YOURSELF "WHAT IF THEY'RE RIGHT?"
ONLY FUNDAMENTALISTS CONTINUALLY REJECT ANY ATTEMPTS TO DISSUADE THEM. CONSIDER NEW VIEWS AND OPINIONS AS IF YOU DIDN'T HAVE ONE OF YOUR OWN.

# 7 Believing is seeing

## How the world is getting better and why many of us miss that

*Both optimists and pessimists contribute to our society. The optimist invents the airplane and the pessimist the parachute.*

– Gil Stern

# My secret world

The turn of the millennium was a particularly depressing time for me. I had broken up from a long relationship. I hated my job. I was in debt. I was in therapy. I wasted time in bad relationships. I was, in other words, stuck in a vicious cycle and, like anyone who has ever been depressed – mildly or clinically – I felt that there was no way out. Many writers and artists have shown that being stuck in such a dark place is an excellent starting point to find another, secret world into which you can escape. Narnia, Middle Earth and Hogwarts, to name but a few. These hidden worlds of the imagination are powerful examples of our collective desire to escape the pain and boredom of the present. Yet very few of us are able to conjure up images of a better world. Most of us remain stuck in this moment, sighing and remaining dependent on other people to define these worlds for us. The signifying trait of a depression is that the sufferer is convinced that things will never really get better or different. That description could also apply to how a lot of us see the world. Tomorrow is never as good as today, and chances are that it might even be a lot worse. Now – or even a few years ago – is as good as it gets. This chapter will deal will pessimism, its drivers and how they blind us from seeing all the things in life, business and society that get a little bit better all the time.

> The signifying trait of a depression is that the sufferer is convinced that things will never get better

## ● Black and white

Take a look at the picture below and think about what you see.

Most people asked to do this will say that they see an elephant or – rather strangely – a mammoth. There is nothing wrong with saying that you see an elephant, but what's interesting is that very few people talk about what dominates the picture: white space. The greater part of the picture is made up of white space, so a more correct answer, in terms of proportions, is that this is a picture of white space. White space, however, is considered of no importance. The greater part of this book is made up of white space, but it's the black letters which give the book its contents. Our brain is programmed to look for anomalies and deviations. If you made an effort to memorize any random Tuesday afternoon ten years ago you would struggle a lot more than if I asked you to recall when you lost your virginity or the first time you got drunk. Just as

> **We are blind to the things we take for granted and consider ordinary**

fish probably didn't discover water, we are blind to the things we take for granted and consider ordinary.

News exists because of black elephants. Imagine a newscast focused on all the people who weren't murdered in an average day, all the countries that didn't experience a coup, or the vast majority of people who kept their jobs in an economic downturn. News exists to dig out diverging details with a universal appeal. Someone we can relate to. A threat we can take seriously. It could happen to you ...

The problem arises when we see the world of the media as being an accurate portrayal of *everything* happening in the world. Moreover, as people tend to be loss averse – we hate loss more than we love gains – you have a situation whereby more people tend to worry about the future than be optimistic about it. To add to the pessimism, consider the fact that many of us tend to be driven by emotions, especially when thinking about the future. Let me clarify that. Let us assume that we spend, as some have claimed, around 12 per cent of our waking time thinking about the future,[1] about an hour of every eight-hour working day. This hour isn't usually focused but rather spread out over the course of the day. Future thinking may hit us in the shower, on the bus, in

**It's easier to make people believe in an idea than to prove an argument**

a meeting or just as we are about to go to bed in the evening. For most of us, thinking about the future usually takes the shape of a question: "What will happen to my kids when they grow up?" or "When will the next terrorist strike happen?" or "Where is the economy heading?" and so on. Very rarely do we stop, sit down and calculate the actual odds of the next terrorist strike or construct a plausible scenario regarding the future of the next generation. Instead, we just feel an emotion ranging from mild anxiety to deep fear and continue doing what we were doing. It isn't so strange, then, that most people tend to be rather pessimistic in their outlook on the present and future when this type of ad hoc mental masturbation substitutes for constructive future thinking. It's easier to make people believe in an idea than to prove an argument. And why should we be optimistic? In the long run, we are all dead anyway. As economists and philosophers have argued for centuries, our lives are as insignificant to the universe as a separate grain of sand is to a beach, except for a small group of people close to us. All these factors – the nature of news, loss aversion, sloppy future thinking and a death looming somewhere on the horizon – conspire to create a very bleak outlook when people are asked about the future. Part of what we fear might actually be justified.

## ● The case for pessimism

Every generation popularizes the notion that the times they live in are unique. "Nothing like this has ever been seen before!" A logical consequence is that the problems each generation faces – real or imagined – are also unsurpassed. The environmental disasters, economic risks, threats of war or violence and the health issues we face feel a lot more grave today than anything ever faced previously in history. This type of hyperbole is especially popular among journalists and politicians – which gives us a clue as to what the intentions behind making these statements might be. It doesn't matter that people have claimed for millennia that the world is ending and have constantly been proved wrong, since they *might* be right this time around. There may, however, be something useful in these types of doomsday scenarios, even though some of them are clearly wrong. Let us consider some examples of erroneous prophecies before we focus on more constructive pessimistic outlooks.

The first error of faulty doomsday scenarios is to mistake scale for severity. The financial turbulence of 2008 or the tsunami disaster of 2004 are two examples where the epithet "The worst disaster in history" was used to describe the events. That statement is accurate only if by "worst" we mean "affecting more people around the world at the same time". If, on the other hand, by "worst" we mean "most serious/grave/damaging", then we are off by a long shot in terms of injury, suffering and deaths caused. The reason we hear the statement "worst event in history" as a description of many accidents and events nowadays is that the world is more connected than it has ever been before. A massacre, a plane crash or a spectacular murder will reach the global airwaves more quickly. The global migration of people means that there's bound to be a Brit, a Swede or a Czech among the dead or injured, no matter where the incident occurred. The globalization of markets and the financial system means that virtually any movement up or down will be felt in many places simultaneously. The interconnectedness of the world is usually heralded as something good in an upturn, so we shouldn't be surprised when this interconnectedness comes back to haunt us in a downturn. Furthermore, since the media operate like an immune system designed to let only certain things get our attention, we need higher doses in order to react to what we're seeing. Hijackings and terror attacks in the 1970s were small-scale events compared to the mass murders they've developed into recently. A hijacking would not gain nearly the same amount of media attention today if it merely ended in a hostage situation with the plane stuck on the ground – as was most often the case a few decades back – and therefore, this type of hijacking doesn't serve the needs of attention-craving terrorists around the world.

Another mistake people make when commenting negatively on present-day developments is to glorify the past and vilify the present. We have a tendency to use "*post hoc ergo propter hoc*" reasoning (after therefore because of). An example is the tendency of people to claim that reality soap operas like *Big Brother* are an example of declining societal values. As a matter of fact, the only thing *Big Brother* and similar formats signify is the development of new kinds of cameras. The bulky, light-dependent cameras of the 1970s would be impossible to drag into a toilet or hide in a bedroom, so *Big Brother* in 1973 would have been quite dull to watch. Yet many insist that earlier generations were noble and civilized whereas the young of today are interested only in short-term fame and lower-back tattoos. This type of "holier than thou" argument has always permeated the debate when new and old generations clash. It is usually characterized by a "You don't get it" line of argument littered with imprecise and incorrect facts thrown in by both sides.

Some doomsday scenarios can be useful, especially if they serve as a collective alarm signal. Health scares and environmental disasters sometimes serve as wake-up calls to the world in order to make us react and start moving in a new direction. Take the abolition of freon in the 1980s, for example. It doesn't really matter what stance you have taken in the debate about global warming as long as it has made you think about how things are made and whether they can be improved or not. Everything can be made in a better way – cheaper, less toxic, more silent, nicer looking, and so on – and doom-mongers can function as catalysts for improving things. Nonetheless, if we need pessimists to recognize certain problems, we will need optimists to solve them.

> If we need pessimists to recognize certain problems, we need optimists to solve them

## ● Accidental learning

We are made by failure. The houses we live in, the cars we drive and the machines we use are safer than ever because earlier versions crashed and burned.[2] What if we gave up whenever something went wrong? If babies stopped trying to walk because they had fallen over. If space exploration ceased because of a mishap. If peace talks were discontinued because one historical peace agreement had failed. You get the picture. If we stopped trying, all human development would choke and die. We are as dependent on accidents and failures for our development as we are on successes. Unfortunately, the implication is that resources will be squandered, value will be destroyed and people will die. The traces of accidents and failure are everywhere we look. From traffic signs (why where they put there in the first place?) to laws (created to prevent something from happening again) and collective wisdom (don't eat the yellow snow!). Failure makes humanity better off in the long run but it makes our path to the future a lot harder. Succeeding is easy. Easier than failure, anyway. When you succeed at something, you tend to do the same thing over and over again, whereas with a failure, you're forced to analyse what went wrong and try new ways.

This cumbersome way of learning from mistakes makes me optimistic for mankind. Individually and collectively we tend to go astray every now and then. We hang out with people we shouldn't or marry the wrong person. We are oblivious to the harmful effects of new materials. We vote apathetically for some populist party only to watch our country turn into a murderous dictatorship. And so on. What makes me optimistic is that we tend to learn not to repeat the same mistakes, even though some are, sadly, repeated. Take warfare, genocide and violence, for example – three nasty downsides to humanity that seem somewhat innate in the human species since they are repeated a few times every century. Since most societies increasingly put a higher value on people's lives, however, we design, build, plan and legislate for security and against risk-taking and destructivity. International organizations such as the United Nations and the European Union may be flawed and bureaucratic but they ensure that a third world war will be a lot harder to start or – at least – will take new forms compared with previous world wars. Standing in a security line at the airport may be tedious, time consuming and frustrating, but would you rather fly on an aeroplane where no passengers had been checked for weapons?

On a more personal level, most people have some sort of evidence of failure's reward – the career failure or heartbreak that made them

change into another and ultimately better person. Failure is successful as a catalyst because it challenges the status quo. Change happens

**If you want to understand the**
**future, study recent failures**

either when the forces opposing it
are relaxed or the forces working
for it are greater than their opponents. Failure makes both of these

situations more likely, so, to quote a famous futurologist: "If you
want to understand the future, study recent failures."[3]

## ● The case for optimism

Social scientists argue that people are far too optimistic for their own
good. We assume that we are immune to the problems other people
face, such as debt or heart failure, and therefore underestimate many
everyday risks (and, paradoxically, overestimate minuscule risks
such as dying in a plane crash or being hit by lightning). From a
theoretical standpoint, we *shouldn't* be optimistic regarding our own
situation. As this is a book dealing with invisible trends, however,
it is worth pointing out that there are number of underlying, long-
term, abstract developments in the world that give us hope:

*The decline of violence*: Some people live by the illusion that life
was somewhat simpler and more in tune with nature's harmony in
the old days. The reality was that life used to be a lot more grim.
Not only were dirt and disease more widespread, violence played a
greater role in everyday life. It wasn't just that violence was a more
accepted means of settling conflicts. It also played a role in entertainment, where torture and blood sports were common means of
amusement. When we claim that we live in "the century of war" or
"in times of great violence", we are either being myopic or just plain
wrong. Violence has been phased out as a form of entertainment
– bar the odd boxing match and fictional portrayal in movies and
games – and as a universally justified means of solving conflicts. This
trend can be seen globally in all societies that have enjoyed positive

economic growth over time, and economics might be a part of the answer to why this is happening. As technology and economic efficiency make life longer and more pleasant, we put a higher value on life in general and leave behind the barbarous notion that "life is cheap".[4]

*A global mindset*: Why did a former vice-president win the Nobel Peace Prize by talking about the weather? Because he synchronized the world's agendas. International conflict arises when nations have colliding agendas, so when we all need to address the same issue – for example, climate change or economic recession – we have less time for disputes and belligerent action. As the world becomes more interconnected, a new kind

> International conflict arises when nations have colliding agendas

of politics emerges. I call it *globalism*, the idea that global issues are of greater importance than local, national or regional ones. Globalism is largely what has driven politics in the past decade. Examples include the emergence of new technologies, the threat of international terrorism, and the widespread effects of economic turbulence and environmental destruction. These issues force cross-border collaboration and fuse many different nations into a single entity. Imagine what this power entity will be capable of when it's time to deal with the eradication of disease or other pressing concerns. The time will come when globalism has been practised for a few decades and the politicians who grew up with only local politics in mind have been replaced by a new generation.

*Increased intelligence*: A controversial hypothesis called the Flynn Effect claims that humanity is getting more intelligent. The man behind it, Professor James Flynn, has compared the results on IQ tests around the world over the past century and found that the results have indeed improved by a few points every decade. The finding is controversial mainly because the improved scores – which are undisputed – aren't certain to reflect an underlying increase in human intelligence. Let's assume that they are, though. What if we are a more intelligent generation than the ones before us? What if there has never been a more intelligent generation than us? We also have access to more information, more knowledge and more opportunities to communicate with people from around the world than anyone has ever had before in history. Wouldn't there be some reason to believe that we would use this to create something good? Something that was better than what previous generations had created? I would argue that this is what we're witnessing right now. Cars aren't as noisy or poisonous as they were a few decades ago. Popular culture has a greater complexity – from TV series to computer games – than it did before.[5] The sustainability movement – in which designers try to find a way to minimize wear and tear on nature when procuring things – is yet another sign.

It doesn't really matter for the sake of this argument whether you consider these three examples – the decline of violence, globalism and increased intelligence – as valid or flawed. My point is that optimism is needed to solve the problems that pessimists present. We need to practise thinking about things in a positive light, assuming problems are soluble, if society is to evolve in an upward spiral.

## A conspiracy to make things better

There are, in general, four forces that tend to drive societal development both on a macro-scale – the so-called megatrends – and in the short term. They are:

● *Technology*: When previously impossible feats become possible, the world changes. Arthur C. Clarke, the science fiction author, famously claimed that a sufficiently advanced technology would be "indistinguishable from magic". Think of technology as a kind of magic, in other words. Technology needs to work in unison with other forces to be effective in changing the world.

● *Economics*: The best way to understand human behaviour is through economic incentives. The completely rational-minded economic man may not exist, but people's predictable response when certain things increase or decrease in price is still striking. From expensive oil to cheap giga-bytes, price dictates what we will buy, what we will sell and how we will behave.

**When previously impossible feats become possible, the world changes**

● *Consumer emotion*: The first two forces can be seen as the rational side of humanity. If people were robots, all cheap new technolo-gies would have a success rate of 100 per cent, which they don't have. People have an unpredictable, emotional side too. We enjoy many things that aren't quantifiable, from certain colours and musical harmonies to religion and philosophy. If a certain idea is to succeed, it needs to resonate with the emotions of some critical mass of people.

● *Group dynamics*: Think of this as a trail of ants following each other. People are invariably social creatures who copy virtually everything from other people – from their way of dressing to their lifestyles and opinions. These idea viruses – or memes,[6] to use their more scientific name – ensure that some big ideas tend to grow even bigger just because they were big in the first place.

**People copy virtually everything from other people**

These four forces are interlinked and collectively represent a strong argument for seeing the future as a brighter place. The reason, I believe, is that each force has an intrinsic drive to improve itself. Technology tends to get better, cheaper and more reliable over time – from hardened steel to vaccines and computer processors. Similarly, prices tend to be pushed downwards over time, since most people prefer cheap to expensive. Some things will always be considered "more expensive" since price is a relative variable, but as technology improves, prices tend to decline. If we view things over time, this tendency can be seen in the price of food – even though food prices have moved slightly upwards in the early 2000s – and the price of oil. The market price of oil may have doubled several times over the past decade but societal efficiency in oil usage has counterbalanced this effect. You can do a lot more for a lot longer with a pint of oil today than you could in the mid-1900s.

Consumer emotions can sometimes run astray. There have been societies that have terminated themselves by celebrating chastity or poverty. A little greed tends to be good for growth. When many people want tomorrow to be a little bit better than today – through more money, more children or a different kind of coffee – societies have just the right amount of long-term growth to improve conditions for everyone over time. This "everyday greed" is an idea that has been spread and copied around the world for the past few decades. It is not without its problems. The environmental impact is considerable, for example. Yet society benefits a lot more when there's a collective idea of a better tomorrow rather than an idealization of, for example, medieval living.

## ● Strike a balance

It doesn't matter whether the glass is half full or half empty. Both arguments are needed. Optimism and pessimism are a set of beliefs affecting how you will see the world. Presenting a case that will reverse the opinion of an optimist or a pessimist is futile. Besides, neither optimism nor pessimism is the real villain when it comes to hindering effective trendspotting. The biggest problem with our worldview is the human propensity to simplify things. We tend to focus on simple symbols and one-sided

> The biggest problem with our worldview is the propensity to simplify things

arguments when we describe the world. A certain country or person is labelled "good" or "bad". A historical event is remoulded to fit Hollywood dramaturgy. Facts are omitted to create a success story or a story about failure. We also have a tendency to consider the times we live in as immunized against the ills of the past, and many are therefore taken by surprise when new examples of fraudulent pyramid schemes or corporate misbehaviour are uncovered. Simplification causes the most severe kind of blindness.

It is hardly surprising that a white, middle-class Swede like me should be optimistic about the world. If we think of the entire world as an airliner with the different travelling classes representing standards of living, Swedes would be sipping champagne in first class whereas millions of people wouldn't even have got aboard the plane. All the trends presented in this book – which I believe point to a better world – can most likely be used to construct a doomsday scenario. In the first chapter, I wrote about a new kind of capitalism, whereby the individual becomes more powerful than ever. This also means that individuals can wreak more havoc than ever. In the second chapter, I talked about fragmentization and the decline of national borders. Evidence of this can be seen in the new world of organized crime where drugs, arms and trafficking represent the underbelly of globalization. The information inferno described in Chapter 3 alienates people and catapults lies and half-truths into headlines news. And so on. A trendspotter tells stories and storytelling is about reducing information. Reducing information is always a dangerous endeavour since the accuracy of the information becomes blunted and may even turn something that is predominantly truthful into something that more resembles a lie. Striking the balance between storytelling and truth-telling is the ultimate skill for any trendspotter, whether they are cool-hunters, business developers, entrepreneurs, journalists, politicians or just ordinary people like you and me.

# The Trendspotter Mission Manual

Widening your horizons is a constant work in progress. Here are some mind-altering ways in which to do it:

TAKE A SABBATICAL FROM THE NEWS!
MANY PEOPLE SUFFER FROM INFORMATION ANXIETY – A FEAR OF MISSING OUT. BE THE ONE WHO MISSES OUT ON THINGS FOR A LITTLE WHILE. TALK TO PEOPLE AND SPEND TIME READING BOOKS INSTEAD OF CONSUMING NEWS. IT'S BOUND TO CHANGE YOUR WORLDVIEW.

PRACTISE OPTIMISM (IF YOU'RE A PESSIMIST – AND VICE VERSA)!
DEVELOPING A NEW WORLDVIEW IS LIKE LOSING WEIGHT: IT TAKES TIME AND EFFORT. DON'T REVERT TO THE OTHER SIDE, THOUGH. STRIVE TO MASTER BOTH VIEWS AND YOU WILL BE A MASTERFUL TRENDSPOTTER.

DIG OUT POSITIVE STORIES ABOUT THE WORLD!
FINDING OPTIMISTIC STORIES IS A LOT HARDER AND WILL FORCE YOU TO LOOK AT STATISTICS, SPEAK TO HISTORIANS, TRAVEL TO PLACES OTHERS LABEL "HOPELESS". SPREAD THE WORD WHEN YOU FIND THEM!

TAKE DOOMSDAY SCENARIOS AND ALARMISTS SERIOUSLY!
IT DOESN'T MATTER WHETHER YOU THINK THEY'RE RIGHT OR NOT. EMBEDDED IN THEIR ARGUMENT MAY BE THINGS THAT WILL MAKE THINGS BETTER.

BEWARE OF THE HALO EFFECT!
SOMETIMES WE REVERE A PERSON AND A COMPANY SO MUCH THAT WE START SEEING THEM AS INFALLIBLE. THAT'S A DANGEROUS VIEW TO HAVE. EVERYTHING HAS A DOWNSIDE. SIMILARLY, THERE'S A "DEVIL'S HORN EFFECT", WHEREBY SOMETHING OR SOMEONE IS CONTINUALLY VILIFIED. NEITHER OF THESE EXTREMIST VIEWS HAS A PLACE IN A BALANCED MIND LIKE YOURS.

# Conclusion

## Everything you know is wrong, right?

Omnia mirari etiam tritissia *(Marvel over everything, especially the most ordinary things)*.

– Carl Linnaeus

# ● Your future just got cancelled

The human brain is a master at filling gaps and making do with the numerous bits and pieces that cross our path daily. It synthesizes these bits into a more or less coherent portrait that we call reality. As we now know, this "reality" is more a function of who we are, where we are and what we are thinking than an accurate portrayal of the world we live in. Just as we have things battling for our attention, our attention also battles for certain things. There are things in the world that we *want* to see because they reflect our values, ideals and experience.

This book has been an attempt to make us aware of some of the pitfalls that we fall into when we try to answer the question "What's going on in the world?" in the hope that awareness is the first step to a remedy. The question then is "Why there should be a remedy?" Why do we need people to achieve a more accurate portrait of the world and the changes it's going through if we are perfectly content to live inside our own bubble of consciousness? The answer is twofold.

First, widening our mental horizons unlocks parts of our brain that will enable us to think new thoughts, dream new dreams and live better lives. For medieval man – with no knowledge of sanitation, antibiotics, dietary needs or a land beyond the horizon – life may have seemed complete, if a bit short. For people living today, life is infinitely better and at least twice as long.

**Understanding other perspectives on the world will turn us into better decision-makers**

Second, understanding other perspectives on the world will turn us into better decision-makers when it comes to making short-term and long-term decisions. People might indeed be motivated by selfish, innate forces, but when we fail to take complex causality into the equation – what happens to security in the First World when oppression and poverty are allowed free rein in the Third World? – the myopic decisions we are bound to make lead us astray. My aim is to make people happier and create better decision-makers.

## Seeing the invisible

Each invisible trend presented in this book has a simple if challenging remedy that we would be wise to practise.

### Invisibility by gradualism *(Too slow to notice)*

Think long term! Chairman Mao famously thought that it was "too early to tell" what the effects of the French Revolution had been. Take a step away from the hustle of daily headlines and hyperbole and look at long-term societal developments to give you a more accurate view of where we are and where we might be heading.

### Invisibility by minuscule changes *(We couldn't see the forest for all those damned trees)*

See without using your eyes! The eye cannot capture atoms moving in a rock. But the hand can. If we touch a rock, we can feel whether it's hot or cold. This temperature, as we know, is the result of the velocity with which the atoms move. In other words, we need to consult other tools if we are to understand how society changes from the bottom up. We need to listen to front-line anecdotes from those who have actually lived the changes themselves. We need to look at the world without the blinkers of history. We need to see things with our own eyes.

### Invisibility by suddenness *(Blink and we miss it)*

Be imaginative! Sudden developments are by nature unexpected. The remedy is simply to anticipate the unexpected by applying more imagination in our foresight. The "what ifs" we come up with need to raise eyebrows and generate "ooohs" and "ahhhs" if they are to be effective.

● **Invisibility by linear thinking** *(Failing to think exponentially)*

Try new things! Similar to sudden trends, quick change generates unexpected results. Exponential change asks us not only to use our imagination but also to relinquish our sense of control. Instead of viewing the world as predictable and controllable, view it as a cauldron of infinite possibilities. Don't travel the beaten path of older generations. The education. The job. The career. Be an explorer and an experimenter instead.

> Quick change generates unexpected results

● **Invisibility by presentism** *(We believe that tomorrow will be like today, more or less)*

Forget today! All we see and know today will be gone some time in the future. Everything you see around you right now will be different. The book. The paper. The language. The people. The stories. Everything.

● **Invisibility by myopia** *(The belief that my world is the world)*

Get out of your head! You've read this book, that's a start. Although we can never leave the confines of our mind or body, we can continually experiment with ways to enrich and complement our perspective. Try to provoke yourself at least once per week.

● **Invisibility by pessimism** *(Since we are all doomed, how can things get better?)*

Never simplify! There's never just *one* way or *one* direction for a certain trend. When everybody cheers, be the inconvenient naysayer, and when everybody is

> When everybody cheers, be the inconvenient naysayer

gloomy, be the shining light that energizes everybody else!

What all this advice points to is ultimately this: dare to think differently! Don't be a fashion victim or a slave to current trends but dare to tell different stories. Inconvenient stories. Complex stories. Your story. We are the generation that trusts our eyes instead of our elders.[1] As psychologist Roger C. Schank puts it: "In bygone days we lived in groups that had wise men (and women) who told stories to younger people if they thought that those stories might be relevant to their needs. This was called wisdom and teaching and it served as a way of passing one generation's experiences to the next."[2] We are no longer slaves to the shackles of inherited "wisdom" but are free to challenge anything. Being deviant

**Like-minded people are the most dangerous force in the world**

is a force for good. Like-minded people are the most dangerous force in the world – unimaginative bankers who blindly copy their risk strategies from competitors or religious zealots with the wrong idea about what will get them into paradise. Assume that everything you know is wrong, and a rampant curiosity will lead you to new and better answer.

## ● The eternal mystery

Atlantis, Eldorado, Outer Space and the Future. The unknown is the source of all imagination. For as long as mankind has been conscious, there have been realms that our psyche cannot reach. Dark forests, inexplicable natural phenomena, extraordinary human abilities, sudden catastrophes, doom and epidemics have separately and collectively titillated and terrorized mankind throughout history. They have spawned religious faiths and scientific inquiry to combat or explain them. They have inspired the arts, created and dethroned rulers, oppressed entire civilizations and set them free.

The unknown is truly an awesome force. Few unknown realms have stimulated our fantasy quite like the Future. From the Oracle at Delphi to science fiction movies, foresight has been a powerful, valuable and highly questionable skill. Powerful because it can change people's behaviour and thereby alter the future. Valuable because we have been willing to pay dearly for future scenarios, whether they came as tarot cards or James Cameron movies. Questionable because the Future is a place that will forever lie ahead of us by its very definition. As soon as the mythical Future reaches us, it's transformed into the more mundane and dull present, only to slide quickly into the oblivion of the past. This impossible equation – reaching the unattainable Future – is what gives the Future its addictive lustre. Like an eternal carrot on a stick, it hovers right in front of us. So close yet so far away, to quote 1980s rockers Hall & Oates.

> Few unknown realms have stimulated our fantasy quite like the Future

It's obvious that the Future isn't merely the name given to a time that lies ahead of us. The Future is a place where our best dreams or worst nightmares come true – a vision of what could be.

Far too many people see themselves as idle passengers on a train that rolls down the one-way track to tomorrow. The driver is elsewhere. We can take small precautions like flossing or jogging to avoid certain future scenarios of the personal kind, but as a collective – a society, an organization – we seem condemned to follow the track laid out before us. The forces that bend, shape and steer the road ahead are just too large for us to comprehend or control. Many of us travel to this *terra incognita* in the dark with our hands tied.

> The Future is a place where our best dreams or worst nightmares come true

I believe that thinking is for doing. We are endowed with a brain built for future thinking in the hope that we can do things about the times that lie ahead. Act upon the insights you get. Change yourself and those around you.

Ultimately, being aware of change blindness may be our best tool for seeing the world as it is and will be. To quote Nobel laureate and poet Wislawa Szymborska: "Whatever inspiration is, it's born from a continuous 'I don't know'."[3]

# Notes

## 1 Blinded by slow motion

1. This fomulation is by archaeologist Timothy Taylor and was retrieved from http://www.truetalkblog.com/truetalk/2009/01/culture-is-all.html on 24 January 2009.

2. The diagram is from *The World Wealth Report*, 2003 edition, published by Merrill Lynch. Retrieved from http://www.ml.com/media/39881.pdf on 1 November 2008.

3. Del Jones, "'Forbes': Facebook CEO is youngest self-made billionaire", *USA Today*, 5 March 2008. Retrieved from http://www.usatoday.com/money/2008–03–05-forbes-billionaires_N.htm on 6 June 2008.

4. John Schwartz, "Dreamers and doers", *New York Times*, 4 January 2009. Retrieved from http://www.nytimes.com/2009/01/04/education/edlife/innovationmain-t.html?ref=edlife on 4 January 2009.

5. Douglas McGray, "Japan's Gross National Cool", *Foreign Policy*, May/June 2002. Retrieved from http://www.chass.utoronto.ca/~ikalmar/illustex/japfpmcgray.htm on 1 May 2008.

## 2 Seeing through the matrix

1. Kevin Kelly, "A new kind of mind", published as a part of Edge's World Question Center, 2009. Retrieved from http://www.edge.org/q2009/q09_1.html#kelly on 23 January 2009.

2. Definition retrieved from http://changingminds.org/explanations/trust/swift_trust.htm on 1 December 2008.

## 3  A shock to the senses

1. Figure taken from presentation by Proact IT, Lund, Sweden, 24 September 2009.

2. This example from Clay Shirky, *Here Comes Everybody*, Penguin, 2009, p. 149.

3. The Croatian tourism example from Rickard Swartz, "Kustens turistparadis Kroatiens nya front", *Svenska Dagbladet*, 27 August 2006. Retrieved from http://www.svd.se/nyheter/utrikes/artikel_347624.svd on 1 August 2008.

4. Moore's Law describes a long-term trend in the history of computing hardware. Since the invention of the integrated circuit in 1958, the number of transistors that can be placed inexpensively on an integrated circuit has increased exponentially, doubling approximately every two years (from Wikipedia).

5. Lee Gomes, "Why we're powerless to resist grazing on endless Web data", *Wall Street Journal*, 12 March 2008. Retrieved from http://online.wsj.com/public/article/SB120527756506928579–3wNdJRXhkpLqY4EDBt4 j31y1fo0_20090312.html?mod=rss_free on 30 June 2008.

6. Example from http://www.rrcap.unep.org/reports/soe/maldives_air.pdf retrieved on 10 October 2008.

7. Farhad Manjoo, "Rumor's reasons", *New York Times*, 16 March 2008. Retrieved from http://www.nytimes.com/2008/03/16/magazine/16wwln-idealab-t.html on 10 November 2008.

8. Coined by Nick Davies in *Flat Earth News*, Chatto & Windus, London, 2008.

9. "The phone of the future", *The Economist*, 30 November 2006. Retrieved from http://www.economist.com/science/tq/displaystory.cfm?story_id=E1_RPTNNGD on 1 March 2009.

10. Jonathan Haidt, *The Happiness Hypothesis*, Random House, London, 2006, p. ix.

## 4  The trend illusion

1. Lowell Bryan and Diana Farrell, "Leading through uncertainty", *McKinsey Quarterly*, December 2008. Retrieved from http://www.

mckinseyquarterly.com/Leading_through_uncertainty_2263 on 27 February 2009.

2. Disclosed by Niklas Bergman, Lecture for Connect Sweden, Stockholm, 23 April 2009.

3. Usually attributed to philosopher Ernst Pöppel. Retrieved from http://query.nytimes.com/gst/fullpage.html?res=940DE7DA173FF934A15750Co A96E948260.

4. Jimmy Guterman, "Release 2.0.2: Web 2.0 meets Wall Street", O'Reilly Radar, 23 May 2007. Retrieved from http://radar.oreilly.com/2007/05/release-202-web-20-meets-wall.html on 1 March 2009.

5. Saul Hansell, "Google keeps tweaking its search engine", *New York Times*, 3 June 2007. Retrieved from http://www.nytimes.com/2007/06/03/business/yourmoney/03google.html on 10 December 2008.

6. Example of Black Mountain School of the Arts taken from Warren Bennis and Patricia Ward Biederman (1997), *Organizing Genius: The Secrets of Creative Collaboration*, Basic Books, 1997.

7. Retrieved from http://www.bbc.co.uk/dna/h2g2/A813962 on 1 January 2009.

8. Retrieved from http://www.ddb.com/pdf/bernbach.pdf on 6 November 2008.

9. Mark Roy, "Pentagon folds hand in online terrorism futures scheme", Internetnews.com, 29 July 2003. Retrieved from http://www.internetnews.com/bus-news/article.php/2241421 on 30 December 2008.

## 5  Beyond the horizon

1. Statistics taken from J. Oeppen and J. W. Vanpel, "Broken limits to life expectancy", *Science*, 296, 1029–1031 (2002), retrieved from http://conservationfinance.wordpress.com/2006/11/05/demography-is-destiny on 19 June 2008.

2. Guy Brown, "Long life's journey into death", *Times Higher Education Supplement*, 7 December 2007. Retrieved from http://www.timeshighereducation.co.uk/story.asp?storyCode=311396&sectioncode=26 on 30 December 2008.

3. Mark Pagel, "We differ more than we thought", Edge's World Question

Center, 2008. Retrieved from http://www.edge.org/q2008/q08_2. html#pagel on 10 January 2008.

4. Tom Teodorczuk, "The shape of things to come", *Guardian*, 5 January 2009. Retrieved from http://www.guardian.co.uk/media/2009/jan/05/ clay-shirky-future-newspapers-digital-media on 6 January 2009.

5. Alex Shakar, *The Savage Girl*, Harper Perennial, 2002.

## 6 Missing the bigger picture

1. Kevin Kelly, "A new kind of mind", Edge's World Question Center, 2009. Retrieved from http://www.kk.org/thetechnium/archives/2009/01/a_ new_kind_of_m.php on 1 March 2009.

2. Retrieved from http://www.brainyquote.com/quotes/keywords/ dimensions.html.

3. Retrieved from http://en.wikipedia.org/wiki/Torn_(Ednaswap_song).

4. Example taken from Stephen Dowling, "What makes a man wear a hat?", *BBC News Magazine*, 1 June 2009. Retrieved from http://news.bbc. co.uk/2/hi/uk_news/magazine/8074663.stm on 2 June 2009.

## 7 Believing is seeing

1. Figure taken from Daniel Gilbert, *Stumbling on Happiness*, Vintage, 2007.

2. This line of reasoning is from Richard Saul Wurman in an interview conducted by Remo. Retrieved from http://www.youtube.com/ watch?v=3dg1Mj4Kyag on 1 March 2009.

3. Quote from Paul Saffo, Institute for the Future.

4. This line of reasoning from Steven Pinker, Speech at TED, Monterey, 7 March 2007.

5. This line of reasoning from Steven Johnson, *Everything Bad Is Good for You*, Riverhead Trade, 2006.

6. A word coined by Richard Dawkins in *The Selfish Gene*, 30th anniversary edn, Oxford University Press, USA, 2006.

## Conclusion

1. Quote from Daniel Gilbert, interviewed online.

2. http://www.edge.org/q2009/q09_print.html#schank.

3. Retrieved from http://nobelprize.org/nobel_prizes/literature/ laureates/1996/szymborska-lecture.html on 1 October 2008.

# Acknowledgements

Thank you!

Peter Fisk – for giving me the idea of writing a book with my thoughts.

Simon Benham – for leading me through the jungle of publishers to find a safe haven.

Martin Liu and Marshall Cavendish – for taking a chance on this book.

Pom, Paul, Gustav and Lotta – for wrapping my words in art.

Tobias and Fredrik – for scrutinizing the text ... twice.

To my family – especially my beloved wife Vesna – who have supported me spiritually and pragmatically over the years to get my thoughts on to paper.

# About the author

**Magnus Lindkvist** is a trendspotter and futurologist based in Stockholm, Sweden. His company, Pattern Recognition, works with companies and organizations around the world to make sense (and money) out of the future.